Lectures on the Gospel of John

Footsteps
of the Lord

Volume 1

Dr. Jaerock Lee

Lectures on the Gospel of John

Footsteps *of the* *Lord*

Volume 1

Dr. Jaerock Lee

FOOTSTEPS OF THE LORD Volume 1:
LECTURES ON THE GOSPEL OF JOHN by Rev. Jaerock Lee
Published by Urim Books (Representative: Kyungtae Noh)
73, Yeouidaebangro 22 Gil, Dongjak Gu, Seoul, Korea
www.urimbooks.com

ISBN: 978-89-7557-605-8, ISBN: 978-89-7557-604-1(set)

Previously published into Korean by Urim Books in 2009

First Published June 2012

Edited by Dr. Geumsun Vin
Designed by Editorial Bureau of Urim Books
For more information contact: urimbook@hotmail.com

Following In His Footsteps...

While retracing the Lord's footsteps during my pilgrimage to the Holy Land, I came upon the blue waters of the Sea of Galilee. I felt as if I had traveled back 2,000 years to our Lord's time. I could neither pass by one pebble, nor one strand of grass without being awed by its significance. Whenever I closed my eyes for a few seconds, it was like I could clearly hear the Lord's voice. And, while watching the trail of dust rise from behind the feet of the pilgrims taking their steps to follow the Lord's steps, the past and the present became tangled together in one mesh, and I felt as if I was standing in the very place where the Lord carried out His ministry. Perhaps this was due to my earnest desire to follow in His footsteps.

There are Four Gospels in the Bible that trace the steps that the Lord took during His ministry. These Gospels are:

Matthew, Mark, Luke and John. Among the Four Gospels, the Gospel of John, written by John—who was so close to the Lord that he was called "The Beloved Disciple," and who encountered everything firsthand—carries the deepest spiritual significance. It is the Gospel of John that most clearly shows that salvation comes from Jesus Christ alone and that He is the true Son of God.

Every time I read the Gospels, I become overwhelmed with emotions. Especially when I read the Gospel of John, and the Holy Spirit enlightens me with the deep spiritual meaning of the Words recorded in it, I cannot help but share this with everyone I know. Just as the Lord asked the apostle Peter to "Feed My sheep," I also felt compelled to feed all believers with the deep, spiritual secrets found in the Gospel of John. This is why in July of 1990 I began giving the 221 sermon series on the Gospel of John.

Lectures on the Gospel of John: Footsteps of the Lord I & II distinctly capture the image of Jesus from 2,000 years ago, as seen in the eyes of John, who witnessed the life of Jesus firsthand. And passing through the time of eternity, the secrets about the beginning of time, as well as information about the origin of Jesus, and about His love and providence that ultimately led to our salvation, are all unraveled.

Whether He was in the Temple, the meeting place, or the mountains or the fields, Jesus taught the people using illustrations from everyday life so that anyone could easily understand Him. His messages were mainly about God, His duty as the Savior, and eternal life. Even though the high priest or the Pharisees couldn't understand the spiritual meaning of His messages, good people like Nicodemus, the Samaritan woman at the well at Sychar, and Lazarus found new lives through the Lord's messages. While sharing messages of life that couldn't be heard anywhere else, the Lord brought consolation and hope to the sick, the poor, and the neglected. However, those people who refused to understand God's love turned their backs against Jesus, because He was unlike the messiah they were waiting for. And ultimately, these same people shouted for His crucifixion on the cross. Now what do you think was going through Jesus' mind as He hung upon the cross?

When we realize the sacrifice Jesus made—enduring all kinds of pain and torment because the cross was the only way to fulfill God's providence—we can only bow down in humility before Him. From His birth, to the signs and wonders He performed, to the messages He delivered, to His suffering on the cross, and finally to His resurrection, every move Jesus made was significant. When we realize the spiritual meaning behind every incident, we can truly understand the deep love God has for us.

The secret to eternal life that's found in the Gospel of John applies to us today. If we open our hearts and accept the Word with a good heart, we will discover an unbelievable treasure, and if we live according to the Word, God will answer our prayers and give us unbelievable blessings and strength.

I would like to give special thanks to Geumsun Vin, Director of Editorial Bureau and the staff who have so diligently worked hard for the publication of this book, and I hope that everyone that reads this book will experience God's great love. I also pray that as you follow the footsteps of the Lord and live according to His teachings, you will receive the answers to all of your prayers, and that God will bestow upon you incredible blessings from above!

January 2009

Jaerock Lee

How the Gospel of John Came To Be

1. About the Author of the Gospel of John

The author of the Gospel of John is the apostle John. Although there is no mention in the Gospel of John about who its author is, we can easily infer that the author is John. This is because as the Lord's "Beloved Disciple" (John 13:23, 19:26, 20:2, 21:7, 20), John experienced the Lord's life firsthand.

John is the son of Zebedee and Salome, and the younger brother of James. With his brother James, John was one of the first to become Jesus' disciples. Because of his fiery temper, John was called a "Son of Thunder". However, he was so loved by the Lord that He got the chance to witness Jesus' spiritual transformation on the Mount of Transfiguration and the bringing back to life of Jairus' daughter. And after Jesus was captured by the Jews and all the other disciples had fled away in fear, John stayed by the Lord until the moment He died on the cross. And because Jesus saw John's trustworthiness, Jesus entrusted John with the virgin Mary, moments before dying on the cross.

After witnessing Christ's resurrection and receiving the Holy Spirit, John was a changed person. And he dedicated his life to spreading the gospel (Acts 4:13) and spent his last years in Ephesus. Then, during Emperor Domitian's harsh tyranny, John was banished to the Island of Patmos. Made entirely of granite, Patmos Island is a barren land where drinking water is scarce and vegetation can hardly grow.

During the day, under the scrutiny of Roman soldiers, John was forced to work in a quarry under harsh conditions. And during the night, while enduring cold and hunger, John put all his energy into prayer. Even now, if we visit the cave where John is said to have prayed every day, we can still see his handprints that tell us how the conditions were while John was there. After Domitian's death, John returned to Ephesus and died there. In his writings, including the Gospel of John, the First, Second, and Third Epistles of John, and the book of Revelation, John mentions about love over 120 times, which is why he is often called the "Apostle of Love".

2. Why the Gospel of John Was Written

In John 20:31, the apostle John clearly states why he wrote the Gospel of John.

"But these are written that you may believe that Jesus is the Christ, the Son of God, and that by believing you may have life in his name."

At that time, many Jews hated Jesus and strongly denied that He was the Christ, ultimately killing Him on the cross. But according to what he witnessed firsthand, the apostle John clearly testified that Jesus is the true Son of God, and that He is the Christ.

The theme of the Gospel of John is "Christ, the love, the life, and the Light of the world". And it tells us about the Christ who came to this world to give us life, the Christ who came to light up the world from the darkness, and the Christ who showed God's love to the world by sacrificing Himself.

3. What Makes the Gospel of John so Special

Generally, the three Gospels that record the ministry and teachings of Jesus—Matthew, Mark and Luke—are similar in content, structure, and perspective; which is why these

Gospels are called the Synoptic Gospels. However, there's definitely something that distinguishes the Gospel of John from the other Gospels.

First, the Synoptic Gospels record the ministry of Jesus with Galilee being the main scene of events, but the Gospel of John records the ministry of Jesus focusing mainly on Jerusalem and Judea.

Secondly, although the Passover is only mentioned once in the Synoptic Gospels (Matthew 26:1-5; Mark 14:1; and Luke 22:1-2), the Gospel of John mentions the Passover three times (John 2:13, 6:4, and 11:55), signifying that Jesus' ministry lasted a total of three years.

Thirdly, if the Synoptic Gospels focus on the kingdom of Heaven, the Gospel of John focuses on the relationship between Jesus and God, and eternal life (John 3:16; 5:24, 11:25, 17:2-3).

The Gospel of John explains about the origin of Jesus Christ and how He was with God from the beginning, and the phrase "I am ---" shows up many times throughout the Gospel of John. Phrases like, *"I am the bread of life"* (John 6:35), *"I am the Light of the world"* (John 8:12), *"I am the way and the truth and the life"* (John 14:6), *"I am the good shepherd"* (John 10:11), and *"I am the true vine"* (John

15:1) shows clearly who Jesus is. And events like the first sign Jesus performed at the wedding feast in Cana, or His visit to Samaria, and many others that are not recorded in the Synoptic Gospels are recorded in the Gospel of John.

Especially in the Gospel of John, we see a record of how Jesus says, *"Truly, truly, I say to you,"* in many occasions. This strongly emphasizes to the reader the absolute value of God's Word.

Table of Contents

Author's Note

Foreword

Table of Contents

Chapter 1

The Son of God
Who Came to This World

Jesus, the Word That Became Flesh

Since the beginning of the world, people have always considered one's family line or lineage as an important factor of life. Family trees show people's desire to discover and cherish their origin and root. A family tree shows who our parents are, who our grandparents are, and who our great grandparents are. If we continue going up the family tree to the very top, to the very origin of all our families, who do you think is the root of all of us? They are Adam and Eve, the progenitors of all mankind.

So what events occurred before the existence of man, how did man come into existence, and why did Jesus, the Son of God, have to come into this world?

God and the Word

"In the beginning was the Word, and the Word was with God, and the Word was God." (1:1)

The secret to the origin of life is found in John 1:1. It says that in the beginning was the "Word." Here, the "Word" stands for God, who exists in the form of the Word. Unlike man, God did not come into existence as a result of being born of parents. He is a perfect Being who solely existed since before the eternity (Exodus 3:14).

In reality, when explaining about God, we don't really need to use the word "beginning." However, the reason we use the word "beginning" is because according to man's knowledge and experience, all things and events must have a starting point. So this word helps us better understand the concept of God.

The word "beginning" is also found in Genesis 1:1, *"In the beginning God created the heavens and the earth."* But this "beginning" is different from the "beginning" written in John. These two "beginnings" each refer to a different time. The "beginning" mentioned in Genesis refers to the time when God created the heavens and the earth, and the "beginning" mentioned in John refers to the time before the eternity that man cannot fathom.

Then why does John say in the beginning was the "Word", and not "God"? This is in order to better explain about the image of God. In the very beginning, God did not exist with the form and appearance of man. As it is written in 1 John

1:5, *"God is Light,"* God governed the entire expanse of time and space in the midst of clear, splendid, and beautiful Light, harboring a myriad of words.

These words are clear, transparent, smooth, and yet majestic and resounding sounds that are strong enough to reverberate through the entire universe. People who have heard God's voice under the profoundly deep inspiration of the Holy Spirit can possibly comprehend this sound. While governing the vast spiritual space alone, at some point, in order to have true children whom He could share true love with, God conceived a plan to "cultivate man."

After planning the cultivation of man, God took on a form for Himself (Genesis 1:26). The God who only existed in the form of the Word now came to have the appearance of man, and He existed as the Triune God, being the Father, the Son, and the Holy Spirit. God had to make Himself into God the Trinity because He needed the Son Jesus, who would become the Savior through whom men could become true children of God, and the Holy Spirit, who would complete the cultivation of man.

Because it is written, "And the Word was with God," it seems as if the Word and God are separate entities. However, it concludes, "And the Word was God" letting us know that the Word is actually God Himself. But if we were to analyze the sequence, the Word was first. This is because the Word became the Trinity, and then took on the name of "God". When the Word existed alone, He did not need any name, but after planning for the cultivation of man, He needed to give man a name to call Him by.

Normally, when we say the "Word", we think of the 66 books of the Bible. But the Bible is a record explaining the position of man, the way of salvation, and so forth—information needed during the time that man is cultivated. However, this is only a small portion of the Word that existed from the very beginning which captures God's entire heart.

Jesus Christ

> "He was in the beginning with God. All things came into being through Him, and apart from Him nothing came into being that has come into being. In Him was life, and the life was the Light of men. The Light shines in the darkness, and the darkness did not comprehend it." (1:2-5)

God, who existed in the form of the Word, made Himself into the Triune God for the cultivation of man, and as the Trinity, He began the work of creation. So this verse tells us that from the very beginning, or even before creation, the Father, the Son, and the Holy Spirit existed together and worked together.

When the time came, God, who had planned for the cultivation of man in order to gain true children, began creating the universe with His Words. When God said, "Let there be light," there was light, and everything in nature, all vegetation and all living organisms, were formed according to His every command (Genesis chapter 1). This is because the Word is God Himself, and the very source of life.

Lastly, God created man, and laid the final foundation for the cultivation of mankind. Through this, God hoped to have children in His own image, but people didn't live according to God's Word. Ultimately, mankind began walking in the way of death.

So, in order to give them true life, God took on flesh like a man and came into this world. This is God the Son, Jesus. Because Jesus has the same origin as God the Father, all of His words and actions show the heart of God. That is why He said, *"He who has seen Me has seen the Father"* (John 14:9).

Jesus had a body of a man, but because He is originally the Word, He was able to heal the sick, raise the dead to life, and calm the wind and the seas (Mark 4:39). And finally, in order to give us Heaven, He took up the cross in our place and gave us eternal life (1 John 1:2).

1 John 5:12 says, *"He who has the Son has the life; he who does not have the Son of God does not have the life."* And in John 14:6 Jesus says, *"I am the way, and the truth, and the life; no one comes to the Father but through Me."*

So Jesus, who is life Himself, came to this world as the Light of man. And because this Light shines in the darkness, man can realize the untruth that lies in the darkness and come to understand true goodness, and walk toward the life, truth, and the Light.

However, as it is written, "the darkness did not comprehend it," people who are soiled in sin are of the enemy devil, who holds authority over the world of darkness. Therefore people under this authority see the Light but cannot understand it.

A Witness to the Light

"There came a man sent from God, whose name was John. He came as a witness, to testify about the Light, so that all might believe through him. He was not the Light, but he came to testify about the Light." (John 1:6-8)

Before sending Jesus to this world and the people living in the midst of lawlessness, immorality, and sin, God prepared a witness to testify about Jesus, who is the Light and the life.

People easily say that God is the one in control over life and death. Of course God has complete authority over life and death and with precision and order He controls the entire universe. However, He does not decide what kind of children are born to what kind of parents. Each man and woman has the free will to choose their spouse, get married, and have children. The only thing God provides is the biological necessities built in their bodies to make their offspring. They are the eggs and sperm.

However, there are exceptional cases where God intervenes in the making of a special person in order to use him in a special way for His kingdom. While preparing to fulfill a certain will in the future, He chooses a certain person for a certain purpose. John the Baptist is such a person. He was conceived under God's providence to prepare the way for Jesus, who was to become the Savior of all mankind.

Luke 1:5-6 says, *"In the days of Herod, king of Judea,*

there was a priest named Zacharias, of the division of Abijah; and he had a wife from the daughters of Aaron, and her name was Elizabeth. They were both righteous in the sight of God, walking blamelessly in all the commandments and requirements of the Lord." Zechariah and Elizabeth were recognized by God as blameless and righteous. The only thing they lacked until their old age was a child of their own. But God saw the goodness of their hearts and blessed Elizabeth's womb so she could conceive a child (Luke 1:13). This child was John the Baptist.

Under God's providence, John, who was born six months before Jesus, led a very special life unlike others. Set apart from the rest of the world, John lived in the wilderness, wearing clothing made of camel's hair with a leather belt around his waist, and he lived on locusts and wild honey. He only communicated with God, and realizing his mission, he prepared for that mission.

His mission was to prepare the way for Jesus. It's much more persuasive when someone else says, "This person is like this," about a certain individual, rather than the individual himself saying, "I am like this." With this in mind, it would have been harder for people to accept Jesus as their Messiah if He had spoken of Himself saying, "I am the Messiah. Believe in Me." This is why God chose John to witness about "The Messiah" who was to come.

If the witness was living in darkness and testifying about the Light, people would never believe him or follow him. This is why John was so upright and unworldly—to the point of owning only one set of clothing—and he led a life in complete obedience to God as he testified about Jesus.

The True Light and the Children of God

"There was the true Light which, coming into the world, enlightens every man. He was in the world, and the world was made through Him, and the world did not know Him. He came to His own, and those who were His own did not receive Him. But as many as received Him, to them He gave the right to become children of God, even to those who believe in His name, who were born, not of blood nor of the will of the flesh nor of the will of man, but of God." (1:9-13)

An object that gives off light, no matter how bright, has its limitations. Even the sun cannot light up the entire earth at one time. However, Jesus is the true Light that gives light to the whole world and everyone in it. Physical light that we see with our eyes can fade away over time, but Jesus Christ is eternal, therefore He is called the true Light.

John the Baptist put his whole life into letting the people know about this Light, but people still didn't recognize this Jesus. This is because Jesus didn't appear anything like the Messiah they had pictured and expected. At this time, the Jews were living under the oppression of the Roman Empire, so they were expecting a Messiah with the political power to free them from this oppression. However, in their eyes, Jesus appeared too powerless and poor for this task.

But to those who accept this Jesus who came to the land of Judea and to those who believe in His name, God gives them the right to become His children. He also gives them the Holy Spirit as a gift and records their names in the Book of Life in Heaven. From that moment forth, they receive the right to call God their "Father". This right is incomparable to anything of this world. Family relationships, or relationships connected by blood end when a person dies. However, spiritual family relationships are eternal, because they stay connected even in Heaven (Matthew 12:50).

So people who become children of God are all brothers and sisters in Christ. Some people think they accepted Christ and came to church all on their own, but this is not so. We do not become God's children through our own efforts or wishes. Only God has control over this, therefore all children of God are born of God.

The Glory of God's Only Begotten Son

> "And the Word became flesh, and dwelt among us, and we saw His glory, glory as of the only begotten from the Father, full of grace and truth." (1:14)

God, who in the very beginning existed as the Word, took on the form of man and came into this world in order to show Himself to us. When He is in the image of His creation to save them, we call Him "Jesus, God's only begotten Son." So the name Jesus means *"He will save His people from their sins"* (Matthew 1:21). Before sending His Son, God sent the angel Gabriel to the Virgin Mary to let her know about Jesus' coming.

"The Holy Spirit will come upon you, and the power of the Most High will overshadow you; and for that reason the holy Child shall be called the Son of God." *(Luke 1:35)*

The physical environment and conditions surrounding Jesus' birth were very poor. At that time, in accordance with the Roman Emperor's decree, Mary and Joseph had to return to their hometown of Bethlehem to register their family in a census. Since all the people who were dispersed all over the land were returning to their hometown all at once, it was no wonder every inn was full. This is why Jesus was born in a stable where animals stay. It means He came to save a people who were no different from the animals He was born next to.

However, the spiritual atmosphere at the time of His birth was anything but poor. Countless angels were praising God and celebrating the birth of the Savior. They knew that Jesus would overcome the power of death and darkness to turn the lost people of this world into God's children again.

Jesus was born in the region of Bethlehem in the land of Judea. But, his family had to flee to Egypt with Him. He spent His early childhood in Nazareth, a region southwest of the Sea of Galilee. Nestled in a quiet and secluded part of nature, Jesus delved into, and became aware of God's will and providence. Whenever He had time, He went to the hills and prayed and meditated on God's Word while looking up toward Heaven. He patiently waited to fulfill His mission of spreading the gospel of Heaven and taking up the cross for mankind's salvation.

When He was 12, Jesus and Mary and Joseph went up to Jerusalem to celebrate the Passover Feast. After the celebration was over Mary and Joseph were getting ready to head back home. There were so many people that they didn't realize that Jesus was missing until after a full day of travel had passed. Thinking that the young Jesus was lost in a strange place, they searched everywhere trying to find Him. They searched the roads and inside the city walls for four days, but couldn't find Jesus anywhere. When they had become tired and on the verge of despair, they saw Jesus in the temple talking with the great teachers of the Law. Jesus didn't appear the least bit distracted or nervous. Rather, He appeared very comfortable and at peace, as if He was in His own home.

For several days, while Jesus was conversing with the teachers of the Law, people who heard Him were amazed by His wisdom and knowledge. This incident shows us how at only the age of 12 Jesus was already very knowledgeable about the Law. Even at this early age, Jesus was already keen on the deep spiritual meanings contained in each law. So it says in Luke 2:52, *"And Jesus kept increasing in wisdom and stature, and in favor with God and men."*

Some people think that as a child, Jesus helped Joseph with carpentry work. But if Jesus had worked with Joseph with his carpentry work, then how could He have had time to become so knowledgeable about the Law to even amaze the great teachers of the Law? And, the Virgin Mary knew who Jesus was. Knowing He was the Son of the Most High God, she would not have allowed Him to do carpentry work. She would have served Him and watched over Him very carefully.

Since He was preparing for His ministry from an early age, the moment He turned 30, He began His ministry with full force. He called His disciples together and showed God's power to the people. As the Son of God, Jesus testified about the living God and gave Him glory. He opened the eyes of the blind, made the mute speak, and brought the dead back to life. To the people who had totally lost their place as the ones created in God's image, and who were living like animals, Jesus showed them their rightful image and identity as children of God. He redeemed people from poverty, diseases, and infirmities. He brought hope to those in despair, and to a people walking toward eternal death, He brought favor and the chance to gain eternal life. This favor that God granted us for free is called "grace".

And the righteous way, life and eternal life, something that never changes, even with the passage of time, we call "truth". Even though Jesus had the same infinite power and authority as God, He treated evil people with goodness and He had mercy on all people—forgiving them and loving them. And because He was lighting the world with this beautiful truth, the Bible says He was full of "grace and truth."

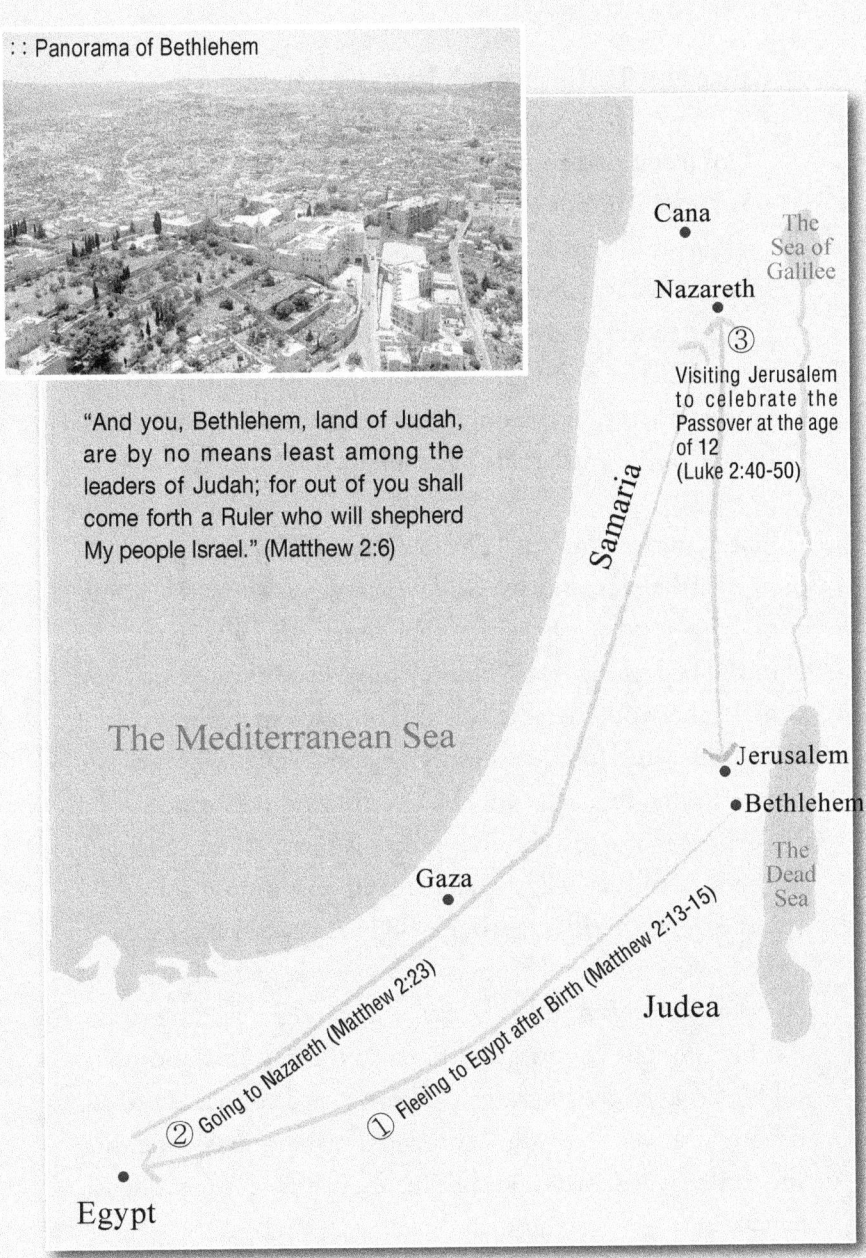

:: Panorama of Bethlehem

"And you, Bethlehem, land of Judah, are by no means least among the leaders of Judah; for out of you shall come forth a Ruler who will shepherd My people Israel." (Matthew 2:6)

Cana

The Sea of Galilee

Nazareth

③

Visiting Jerusalem to celebrate the Passover at the age of 12 (Luke 2:40-50)

Samaria

The Mediterranean Sea

Jerusalem

Bethlehem

The Dead Sea

Gaza

② Going to Nazareth (Matthew 2:23)

① Fleeing to Egypt after Birth (Matthew 2:13-15)

Judea

Egypt

:: The Birth and Development of Jesus

Grace and Truth through Jesus Christ

"John testified about Him and cried out, saying, 'This was He of whom I said, "He who comes after me has a higher rank than I, for He existed before me."' For of His fullness we have all received, and grace upon grace. For the Law was given through Moses; grace and truth were realized through Jesus Christ. No one has seen God at any time; the only begotten God who is in the bosom of the Father, He has explained Him." (1:15-18)

The name John means "The loved one of God". John himself knew that he was sent by God before Jesus to testify about Him. This is why John knew that Jesus, who was with God from the beginning, was "before" him. Even though he lived alone in the wilderness he was full of grace with the hope of Heaven. Because John was testifying about Jesus, who was the Light and life, he could only be overflowing with grace. John also expresses the joy abounding in his heart when testifying that because of Jesus we have all received "grace upon grace."

Just as John testifies, anyone who believes and accepts Jesus as the Son of God and repents of his sins is joyful because of the hope of Heaven in his heart. Jesus brought healing to the sick, He brought comfort and hope to the dejected and poor, and He brought the blessing of salvation and eternal life to all. Although He was in the flesh, because He is originally one with God, only Jesus Christ could bring about this grace and truth to mankind.

The Law is a record of the spiritual laws under God's authority that we absolutely need in order to live in this world. In addition to explaining the heart of God in the Law, it also explains the order in which the spiritual world is maintained, and all the rules about blessings, curses, sin and death, judgment, salvation, and all other pertinent information needed for the cultivation of man. The "Torah" in Hebrew, is a book of laws consisting of 613 articles that God gave to the Israelites through Moses before Jesus came into this world. This is why John stated in verse 17, "For the Law was given through Moses; grace and truth were realized through Jesus Christ."

While evangelizing, you occasionally meet people who say, "Show me God. Then I'll believe." However, just because someone asks to see God doesn't mean He can just show up in front of them. This is because since the disobedience of Adam, all men became sinners, and sinners cannot see the face of God; otherwise they will die (Exodus 19:21). That is why the Word, who is God, became flesh and came into this world with the name of Jesus, so that all man could finally see God. Therefore if we believe in this Jesus and live according to His Word, we can meet God, and whatever we ask for, He will give to us.

The Testimony
of John the Baptist

In 433 B.C., after the Prophet Malachi, Israel faces a spiritual "Dark Ages". For 400 years, there was no prophet of God to declare and deliver His messages to the people. As a nation under the subjugation of Rome, Israel was moaning and groaning through a long, silent 400 years when finally a prophet broke through this silence. This prophet was John the Baptist.

The Voice of One Calling in the Wilderness

"This is the testimony of John, when the Jews sent to him priests and Levites from Jerusalem to ask him, 'Who are you?' And he confessed and did not deny, but confessed, 'I am not the Christ.' They asked him, 'What then? Are you Elijah?' And he said, 'I am not.' 'Are you the Prophet?' And he answered, 'No.' Then they said to him, 'Who are you, so that we may give an answer to those who sent us? What do you say about yourself?' He said, 'I am a voice of one crying in the wilderness, "Make straight the way of the Lord," as Isaiah the prophet said.'" (1:19-23)

If we look at Matthew chapter 3, we see John the Baptist in the Wilderness of Judea calling out, *"Repent, for the kingdom of heaven is at hand"* (v. 2). He was shouting this out to tell the people about Jesus, who came as the Savior of the world, and lead people to Him. And when John was baptizing in the Jordan River, people came from Jerusalem and all Judea and the whole region of the Jordan to confess their sins and to be baptized by him.

While John was preparing the way for the Lord in this way, he became a matter of major discussion among the people. Living in the wilderness on only locusts and wild honey, to the Israelites who were in complete spiritual darkness, John appeared to be a single ray of light. As time passed, the word about John the Baptist began to spread, and the Jews became curious about who he was. That is why they sent priests and Levites who were knowledgeable about the laws to question him.

"Who are you?"

"I am not the Christ."

"Are you Elijah?"

"I am not."

"Are you the Prophet?"

"No."

During King Ahab's reign in Northern Kingdom of Israel there was a prophet named Elijah. To prove that the God of Israel was the one true God Elijah entered into contest against 850 prophets of Baal and Asherah. God answered Elijah's request by lighting his sacrifice with fire from heaven, while the opposing prophets received no answer from their gods. Because he was holy and pure, he was lifted up to Heaven without experiencing death. For a very long period of time he was cherished in the hearts of the Israelites and received their love and respect. As it is written in Malachi 4:5, *"Behold, I am going to send you Elijah the prophet before the coming of the great and terrible day of the LORD,"* the Jews believed in this prophecy and eagerly waited for Elijah. But contrary to their hope and wish, John the Baptist clearly denies being the Christ or Elijah.

Finally as a result of their persistent inquiry John the Baptist introduces himself in this way, "I am a voice of one crying in the wilderness, 'Make straight the way of the Lord.'" Because he knew very clearly that his mission was to prepare the way for the Lord, he made sure not to cross any boundaries. And he always declared that the One who is greater than himself is coming after him.

"I Baptize with Water"

"Now they had been sent from the Pharisees. They asked him, and said to him, 'Why then are you baptizing, if you are not the Christ, nor Elijah, nor the Prophet?' John answered them saying, 'I baptize in water, but among you stands One whom you do not know. It is He who comes after me, the thong of whose sandal I am not worthy to untie.' These things took place in Bethany beyond the Jordan, where John was baptizing." (1:24-28)

Of course the high priests and Levites were suspicious and doubtful—their people were being baptized by somebody who claimed not to be either Elijah or a prophet. So they question him, "Why then are you baptizing?" Why do you think John the Baptist baptized with water? He baptized with water in order to let the people know about the coming Messiah.

Spiritually, water symbolizes the water of life that gives eternal life to man, which is, the Word of God. Just as water cleans the body of dirty things, God's Word cleans the soul of sin. John baptized with water in a symbolic way in order to make the people first repent of their sins and then believe and accept the Son of God who was coming as the Savior.

At that time, John the Baptist was highly respected by the people because he was upright and lived according to the Law and he lived in the truth. This man was going about and telling the people about the Messiah, humbling himself, saying, ""It is He who comes after me, the thong of whose sandal I am not worthy to untie." When we consider the fact that many people considered him a prophet and followed him, we can see how humble he was. At the same time, John's confession also helps us realize how holy and valuable Jesus is.

"Behold, the Lamb of God ..."

"The next day he saw Jesus coming to him and said, 'Behold, the Lamb of God who takes away the sin of the world!'" (1:29)

The next day, Jesus went to meet John at the Jordan River. He went to be baptized before officially starting His public ministry. Jesus had no faults or weaknesses. However, He was baptized because He had come into this world in the flesh, in the image of His creation, in order to save them. That is why He made sure to follow the order of this world. So His baptism at the Jordan River was significant because it symbolized the sacrifice and devotion He was about to make by taking up the cross to save countless souls.

In the fullness of the Holy Spirit, the moment John saw Jesus, he said, "Behold, the Lamb of God who takes away the sin of the world!" During their lifetime here on earth, many people either chase after the pleasures of this world, or commit all kinds of different sins while trying to gain fame, power, or just to get ahead of others. John made his confession, knowing that Jesus would eventually be nailed to the cross for all these sins.

Then of all the animals that exist, why did John compare Jesus to a lamb? He made this comparison because of the distinct characteristics of a lamb. Sheep are very obedient, and they go only where their shepherd guides them. Even if someone captures them or shaves their wool, they do not resist. Their wool, milk, and flesh are sacrificed for the benefit of people.

Year-old-male lambs in particular with very soft wool that looked very lovely were used for sacrifice to God. If compared to people, these lambs would be equivalent to young people at the most beautiful stage of their lives. Because this is before the mating age, the lambs are very pure and without defect. This is like Jesus, the sacrificial lamb, who unselfishly gave Himself for us, the sinners. Without any hint of belligerence or ostentation, He was gentle and meek, pure and without any fault.

John compared Jesus to a lamb because this Jesus, like a sacrificial lamb, had to be sacrificed for the sinners as a sin offering. Some people call new believers who are young in faith a "lamb." However, the Bible refers to believers as "sheep" or "God's sheep", but never a "lamb." This is because the term "lamb" is used in reference to Jesus Christ.

The Son of God

"This is He on behalf of whom I said, 'After me comes a Man who has a higher rank than I, for He existed before me.' I did not recognize Him, but so that He might be manifested to Israel, I came baptizing

in water. John testified saying, 'I have seen the Spirit descending as a dove out of heaven, and He remained upon Him.' I did not recognize Him, but He who sent me to baptize in water said to me, 'He upon whom you see the Spirit descending and remaining upon Him, this is the One who baptizes in the Holy Spirit.' I myself have seen, and have testified that this is the Son of God." (1:30-34)

Jesus was born into this world six months after John the Baptist. But spiritually, He had been in existence since before the beginning of time. John knew this truth. This is why he said, "After me comes a Man who has a higher rank than I, for He existed before me."

And he states that the reason for his own existence is to reveal this Jesus to Israel. The reason why John baptized with water was to tell the people about Jesus, who would be baptizing with the Holy Spirit. In order to better understand the baptism by the Holy Spirit which Jesus would be performing later on, people needed to understand the spiritual meaning behind baptism by water first.

God told John the Baptist that the one on which the Spirit comes down upon like a dove from heaven is the Christ. Just as God had spoken, after Jesus was baptized and rose up from the water, heaven opened up, and the Spirit came upon Him like a dove. Seeing this, John the Baptist knew that Jesus was the Son of God. And, Jesus, being the very first to receive the Holy Spirit, He would be the one who would later baptize all the people with the Holy Spirit.

So why do you think the Bible says that the Holy Spirit came down like a dove? A dove symbolizes peace, and it is a very mild and gentle bird that is very friendly with people. But this does not mean that an actual dove came down and landed on Jesus. It means that the Spirit's presence came down upon Jesus in a mild and gentle manner, reflecting Jesus' character. The Holy Spirit works differently, according to each person's temperament. For people with a fiery temperament, the Holy Spirit works in a very strong way; and for people with a gentle temperament, the Holy Spirit works in a soft and gentle way. Because God opened up John's spiritual eyes, he was able to see the Holy Spirit's presence, which people cannot see with their physical eyes. Therefore he was able to see and testify that Jesus was the Son of God.

The Followers of Jesus

When John finally met Jesus, whom he had been waiting for and for whom he had been sent in advance by God, how excited and overwhelmed he must have felt! Upon seeing this Jesus who came to be baptized by him, John was so embarrassed that he tried to turn down His request. However, Jesus says, *"Permit it at this time; for in this way it is fitting for us to fulfill all righteousness"* (Matthew 3:15). Jesus' gentle, yet determined voice persuaded John not to hesitate any longer. This is because everything was happening in accordance with God's will.

The Disciples of John the Baptist

"Again the next day John was standing with two of his disciples, and he looked at Jesus as He walked, and said, 'Behold, the Lamb of God!' The two disciples heard him speak, and they followed Jesus. And Jesus turned and saw them following, and said to them, 'What do you seek?' They said to Him, 'Rabbi (which translated means Teacher), where are You staying?' He said to them, 'Come, and you will see.' So they came and saw where He was staying; and they stayed with Him that day, for it was about the tenth hour." (1:35-39)

It was the day after John the Baptist baptized Jesus with water. John wanted his loving disciples to follow Jesus, the Son of God. That is why John said to his disciples, "Behold, the Lamb of God!" to reiterate once more who Jesus truly was.

So Jesus asked these disciples what they wanted. He didn't ask because He didn't know what they wanted. He asked because He could respond to them only if they asked (Matthew 7:7). He wanted to give them the opportunity to ask. The moment they heard this, the disciples immediately began to follow Jesus.

"What do you seek?"
"Rabbi, where are You staying?"

"Rabbi" in Hebrew is a title for a scholar of the laws of Judaism, and it means "My teacher, my Lord." It is a title used to address a person of respect, or a scholar with lots of knowledge. And once again He spoke to John's disciples, who considered Him their teacher saying, "Come."

While following Jesus and being immersed in conversation with Him, the disciples didn't even realize the passing of time. They were so drawn into His messages.

Andrew and Simon Peter

"One of the two who heard John speak and followed Him, was Andrew, Simon Peter's brother. He found first his own brother Simon and said to him, 'We have found the Messiah' (which translated means Christ). He brought him to Jesus. Jesus looked at him and said, 'You are Simon the son of John; you shall be called Cephas' (which is translated Peter)." (1:40-42)

One of the John's disciples who was following Jesus was Andrew, Simon Peter's brother. While talking with Jesus, he discovered an amazing truth. He discovered that Jesus was the Messiah about whom all the prophecies had predicted! Andrew couldn't hold this news any longer. So he hurried to his brother Simon and said, "We have found the Messiah!"

Can you imagine how Simon must have felt when he saw

Andrew's face all flushed and filled with excitement as he shouted, "I met the Messiah!" Simon might have been a little bewildered at first, but since his brother was confessing to have met the Christ—the very Messiah the Israelites have been eagerly awaiting for all these years—he quickly followed his brother to go see Him. Upon seeing Simon, Jesus said, "You are Simon son of John; you shall be called Cephas (Peter)."

Jesus knew from the beginning who he was, and He saw right through Simon's heart. Jesus also knew how God was going to use him later on. "Cephas", or "Peter", as Jesus called him, would later become Jesus' prized disciple who sacrificed his life to build a strong foundation on which the first church would be built.

The other Gospels report that Peter and Andrew were fishing by the Sea of Galilee when they were called to become Jesus' disciples (Matthew 4:18; Mark 1:16-18). The reason why the Gospel of John is different in this respect is because the Gospel of John is reporting on Andrew and Peter's first meeting with Jesus; not when they were called to be His disciples.

Phillip and Nathanael

"The next day He purposed to go into Galilee, and He found Philip. And Jesus said to him, 'Follow Me.' Now Philip was from Bethsaida, of the city of Andrew and Peter. Philip found Nathanael and said to him,

'We have found Him of whom Moses in the Law and also the Prophets wrote—Jesus of Nazareth, the son of Joseph.' Nathanael said to him, 'Can any good thing come out of Nazareth?' Philip said to him, 'Come and see.'" (1:43-46)

The day after Jesus met Andrew and Peter, as He was about to leave for Galilee, Jesus met Phillip. He said to him, "Follow Me." Phillip, like Peter, was from the town of Bethsaida, and he also was called to be Jesus' disciple. And like Andrew, after finding out that Jesus was the Messiah, he went to share the news with Nathanael. Because at this time Phillip didn't really know much about Jesus, he introduces Him as "Jesus of Nazareth, the son of Joseph". And he said, "We have found Him of whom Moses in the Law and also the Prophets wrote—Jesus of Nazareth, the son of Joseph." But Nathanael asked, "Nazareth! Can any good thing come out of Nazareth?"

Nathanael couldn't believe Phillip. He thought, 'How can the great Messiah possibly come from a small shabby town?' Nathanael thought that the Messiah who would save all mankind from their sins would be, as God's Son, a good person, but also at the same time be so highly esteemed that men wouldn't dare to look at Him with ease. So of course, upon hearing that the Messiah was the son of an ordinary carpenter, he couldn't believe his ears!

Phillip, being a wise man, does not try to argue with Nathanael. He just tells him to simply come and see for himself, if he couldn't believe it. Nathanael had a hard time believing, but because he had a good heart, he listened to his friend's advice and followed him.

> "Jesus saw Nathanael coming to Him, and said of him, 'Behold, an Israelite indeed, in whom there is no deceit!' Nathanael said to Him, 'How do You know me?' Jesus answered and said to him, 'Before Philip called you, when you were under the fig tree, I saw you.'" (John 1:47-48)

When Jesus sees Nathanael walking toward Him after being guided by Phillip, He compliments him saying, "Behold, an Israelite indeed, in whom there is no deceit!" Jesus saw the center of Nathanael's heart, and He knew that he had an unchanging heart—being faithful and obedient to God's Word. So why do you think Jesus called Nathanael "an Israelite indeed"?

When God chose Jacob to become the father of Israel, He wanted a people who were good and true. However, from time to time, the Israelites wandered from God and worshipped other idols. God was searching for a "true Israelite" who was truly faithful and obedient, and that's when Nathanael appeared before Jesus.

Of course Nathanael was surprised when Jesus, who had never met him before, recognized him, and complimented him. He asked, "How do You know me?" Jesus answered, "Before

Philip called you, when you were under the fig tree, I saw you."

Jesus never met Nathanael before, but He was looking right through him! Because Nathanael had a good heart, he didn't doubt Jesus by asking, "I wonder if someone told Jesus about me prior to our meeting?" Instead, he opened his heart and accepted the truth as it was.

Nathanael's Spiritual Confession

"Nathanael answered Him, 'Rabbi, You are the Son of God; You are the King of Israel.' Jesus answered and said to him, 'Because I said to you that I saw you under the fig tree, do you believe? You will see greater things than these.' And He said to him, 'Truly, truly, I say to you, you will see the heavens opened and the angels of God ascending and descending on the Son of Man.'" (1:49-51)

After exchanging just a few words with Jesus, Nathanael made a very surprising confession: "Rabbi, You are the Son of God; You are the King of Israel." To which Jesus replied, "Because I said to you that I saw you under the fig tree, do you believe? You will see greater things than these."

After hearing Nathanael's spiritual confession, Jesus told him about what was to come in the future. Just like Bartholomew, one of Jesus' apostles, Nathanael witnessed many signs and wonders as he kept close by Jesus. He witnessed many people being healed of all kinds of diseases; he witnessed Lazarus coming back to life after being dead and decaying for 4 days; and in the end, he witnessed Jesus dying on the cross, being buried in the tomb, and then resurrecting on the third day.

Jesus then gave Nathanael another blessed message: "Truly, truly, I say to you, you will see the heavens opened and the angels of God ascending and descending on the Son of Man." This is confirmation of Nathanael's confession, "You are the Son of God; You are the King of Israel." The reason why Jesus doesn't reply, "Yes, you are right," and instead indirectly acknowledges Nathanael's confession and indirectly expresses that He is the Messiah is because it was not yet Jesus' time to do so. If He tells everything out in the open, the enemy devil and Satan would distract the plan of salvation and try to prevent God's will from happening. Therefore He didn't want to reveal Himself just yet. Jesus always looked at the center of a person's heart; and keeping in mind the mission He must fulfill, He only acted in complete accordance to God's will.

Chapter 2

Jesus Performs
the First Sign

The Wedding Feast in Cana

As He matured in age, Jesus constantly prepared Himself for His ministry as the Savior and waited for His time to come. And as soon as He turned 30, He officially began His public ministry to save mankind as the Messiah.

The sign Jesus performed while attending the wedding feast in the region of Cana marks the beginning of His public ministry. Some people think that Jesus turned the water into wine to simply bless the people at the banquet. However, there is a special meaning behind this first sign He performed as He began His public ministry. Jesus attending a wedding feast, turning water into wine, and speaking certain words in His conversation with Mary, all hold great meaning.

Jesus Was Invited to a Wedding Banquet

"On the third day there was a wedding in Cana of Galilee, and the mother of Jesus was there; and both Jesus and His disciples were invited to the wedding. When the wine ran out, the mother of Jesus said to Him, 'They have no wine.' And Jesus said to her, 'Woman, what does that have to do with us? My hour has not yet come.'" (2:1-4)

The region of Cana is not far from Nazareth or Galilee. One day, Mary, and of course Jesus and His disciples as well, were invited to a wedding banquet being held there.

If you look at Luke 17:27, it says that during the judgment in Noah's time, *"they were eating, they were drinking, they were marrying, they were being given in marriage, until the day that Noah entered the ark, and the flood came and destroyed them all."* And in verse 30 it says, *"It will be just the same on the day that the Son of Man is revealed."* The words, "eating, drinking, marrying and being given in marriage" were used to explain how the world will be filled with evil in the last days.

Furthermore, Cana in Galilee spiritually symbolizes the world, and the wedding banquet in Cana symbolizes the world filled with eating, drinking, and indulging in sin in the last days. The enemy devil, who is the ruler of this world, tempts people to follow their sinful instincts to become drunk with the secular world.

So why did Jesus attend a secular wedding feast? Jesus would never attend a feast or banquet to indulge in worldly pleasure. He came into this world only to give glory to God and to save mankind. So how could He possibly begin His public ministry by indulging in worldly pleasures? The reason Jesus attended the secular wedding feast was to show that the Son of God, who is holy and set apart from sin, came into a world full of sin to save the sinners in it.

Right when the party was at its peak, all the wine ran out. For the host of the party, it was a very upsetting situation. Mary, who found out what was going on, felt sorry for the host and told Jesus about what had happened. This is because during the thirty years that she had lived with Jesus, she knew that He had the power to do anything. However, Jesus gives Mary an unexpected reply saying, "Woman, what does that have to do with us? My hour has not yet come."

And, why does Jesus call Mary "woman"? God, the Creator of the universe, cannot call a woman who is His creation, "mother." Of course for thirty years He served His physical parents in accordance with the commandments and His duties as son. However, after beginning His ministry, He only carried out His mission as "God's Son." That is why Jesus called Mary "woman" in the presence of His disciples at the banquet.

And the reason He asked Mary, "Woman, what does that have to do with us?" was to show that He and His disciples have no part in the eating, drinking, and merrymaking of men. And what does Jesus mean when He says, "My hour has not yet come"? In this sentence, the word "hour" signifies a spiritual time. So what He means is that the time has not yet come for Him to fulfill His mission of salvation by dying on the cross for our sins yet. Mary was telling Jesus about the physical situation they were in, in which the wine had run out at the banquet, but Jesus was answering her with words that carried deep, spiritual significance.

The Spiritual Significance of the Six Stone Jars

"His mother said to the servants, 'Whatever He says to you, do it.' Now there were six stone waterpots set there for the Jewish custom of purification, containing twenty or thirty gallons each. Jesus said to them, 'Fill the waterpots with water.' So they filled them up to the brim." (2:5-7)

Mary tells the servants to do whatever Jesus tells them to do. Initially, this can lead us to think that Mary's actions go against what Jesus just said when He replied, "My hour has not yet come." However, there is no way that Mary would have disregarded what Jesus said. Even though Jesus said that He has nothing to do with the merry-making of this world, Mary had faith that He would have mercy on the host of the party—who was in a very tough situation—and do something for him.

At the banquet were six stone waterpots that the Jews used for ceremonial washing, each capable of holding twenty to thirty gallons of water. The Bible mentions that the jars were

: : The Wedding at Cana (Painting inside the Franciscan Wedding Church)

: : The Franciscan Wedding Church

made of "stone." This is because a stone represents something that is strong and unchanging, like a firm foundation. This signifies the unchanging promise of God. The fact that there were six stone jars is significant because it represents the 6,000 years of human cultivation. Just like the stone jars, God's providence and love toward mankind was and will be unchanging during the 6,000 years of human cultivation.

When Mary showed Jesus her undeterred faith, Jesus answered her by performing a sign. Jesus told the servants to fill the six jars with water. It says that they filled the jars to the brim, which means it was close to overflowing. The fact that the water came to the brim of the jars but did not overflow signifies that the history of human cultivation will be completed before the end of the 6,000 years. The very small space left above the brims of the jars symbolically represents the events that will occur here on earth during the Seven-year Great Tribulation following the completion of human cultivation.

The Providence of Turning Water into Wine

"And He said to them, 'Draw some out now and take it to the headwaiter.' So they took it to him. When the headwaiter tasted the water which had become wine, and did not know where it came from (but the servants who had drawn the water knew), the headwaiter called the bridegroom, and said to him, 'Every man serves the good wine first, and when the people have drunk freely, then he serves the poorer wine; but you have kept the good wine until now.'" (2:8-10)

When the servants obeyed Jesus; they drew some from the jar and took it to the headwaiter of the banquet, the water had turned into wine! The water that Jesus had turned into wine was a wine that tasted amazingly great. It tasted so good that the headwaiter of the banquet called the bridegroom to ask about it. Usually at a party, people serve their best wine first because, as the party progresses and people become drunk, their senses grow dull, so at this point, it doesn't really matter if the quality of the wine is a little less than before. But at this banquet, the best wine was coming out later, so the headwaiter of the banquet thought it was a little strange.

Jesus did not attend the wedding banquet and turn the water into wine to cause the people to fall deeper into debauchery. Jesus actually created wine that didn't contain any substance that would cause people to become drunk. In order to understand why Jesus performed such a sign, we need to first understand the spiritual significance of water and wine.

Here, the water represents the body of Jesus Christ who came into this world when the Word became flesh (John 1:14), and the wine represents the blood of Jesus who would save all the sinners. Therefore, the reason why Jesus turned water into wine and had people drink it was to show that when the time comes, Jesus would die on the cross and shed His blood so that those people who believe in this would be forgiven of their sins and receive salvation.

The "headwaiter of the banquet" represents the worldly

people who don't believe in God, and the servants who brought the drink to the headwaiter of the banquet represent the servants and workers of God. The servants knew how the wine came to be, but the headwaiter of the banquet had no idea where it came from. Likewise, servants and workers of God know very well that it is by the blood of Jesus that we are saved, so they try to share about Jesus Christ and God's Word to their sheep, as well as the unbelieving people of this world.

Just like the headwaiter of the banquet was joyful when he tasted the new wine, people who are forgiven of their sins by the precious blood of Jesus Christ truly feel joy from the center of their hearts. Their sins would have caused them to go to the way of eternal death, but because of God's grace, their sins were washed away, so of course they will feel great joy!

And the fact that the wine that turned from water tasted good spiritually represents God's Word that is as sweet as honey. People who don't believe in God try to satisfy their physical desires by chasing after all kinds of secular things; however, since they eventually face eternal death, all those things become meaningless. But God's Word is sweet and profound, and it gives us life, so it is truly valuable.

So this first sign showed God's providence in leading His people to Heaven by forgiving them of their sins through the precious blood of Jesus and sanctifying them through His Word.

"This beginning of His signs Jesus did in Cana of Galilee, and manifested His glory, and His disciples

believed in Him." (2:11)

When the Bible says that the disciples put their faith in Jesus after seeing His glory through this first miraculous sign, this doesn't simply refer to this one single event of Jesus turning water into wine. This phrase also symbolically refers to all the events that will fulfill God's providence in the future. In Matthew 12:38-40 we see a scene where some of the Pharisees and teachers of the law come to Jesus and ask Him to show them a sign. Up to that point, by God's power, Jesus had showed enough evidences so people could believe. Jesus healed the blind so they could see, and healed the mute so they could speak. Jesus showed numerous other signs in addition to these; however, they weren't enough for them. They still would not believe, and they asked for yet another sign.

In Matthew 12:39-40, Jesus answered and said to them, *"An evil and adulterous generation craves for a sign; and yet no sign will be given to it but the sign of Jonah the prophet; for just as Jonah was three days and three nights in the belly of the sea monster, so will the Son of Man be three days and three nights in the heart of the earth."* The belly of the sea monster is referred to as "the depth of Sheol" in the Old Testament (Jonah 2:2). What Jesus is saying here, is that just as Jonah disobeyed God and spent three days in the grave, Jesus will also die on the cross for mankind's sins and then go to the grave. And then, He will show us another sign by coming back to life in three days.

So the phrase, "This beginning of His signs Jesus did in Cana of Galilee, and manifested His glory, and His disciples believed in Him," doesn't mean that Jesus' disciples believed the moment they saw the water turning into wine. This phrase is a prophecy that the disciples will gain true faith only after Jesus performs "the sign of Jonah" by dying on the cross and showing the glory of the resurrection. And just as this Scripture stated, only after witnessing the resurrection did the disciples truly understand everything Jesus had told them, and they believed in Him.

"After this He went down to Capernaum, He and His mother and His brothers and His disciples; and they stayed there a few days." (2:12)

After performing His first sign, He went with His mother and brothers and His disciples to Capernaum. Capernaum, located northwest of the Sea of Galilee, was a heavily populated place, because at that time it had a Roman army post, and it was also the center of administration. Jesus also carried out much of His evangelistic ministry at this location.

This is where He called Peter, Andrew, James, and John to be His disciples; and this is where He taught them many things. This is the place where Jesus healed a paralytic and brought back to life Jairus' daughter. However, the people of Capernaum did not accept Jesus' words. The people in this place witnessed more of God's power than the people of any other region, and yet they did not repent. It's no wonder Jesus was grieving for them (Matthew 11:23).

Around the sixth century, the city walls of Capernaum collapsed; and it remains uninhabited and in ruins to this day.

Jesus did not stay in this region for long, and when we look at all He did, we can understand why. Jesus never acted out of His own will. He always followed God's will. He only said what God told Him to say, He only went where God told Him to go, and He only stayed where God told Him to stay.

Stop Making My Father's House a Place of Business

During the reign of King Rehoboam, Solomon's son, Israel was divided into Northern Kingdom of Israel and Southern Kingdom of Judah, and as a result, they experienced many invasions from enemy nations. Later, in 722 B.C., Northern Israel was destroyed by the Assyrians, and in 586 B.C., Southern Judah was invaded by Babylon, and many Israelites were taken as captives. As a result, the Jewish people suffered for many years. However, even under the oppression of the Romans, the Jews managed to return to Jerusalem from all over to make sacrifices to God on their nation's biggest holiday, the Passover.

Jesus Cleans out the Temple

"The Passover of the Jews was near, and Jesus went up
to Jerusalem. And He found in the temple those who
were selling oxen and sheep and doves, and the money
changers seated at their tables. And He made a scourge
of cords, and drove them all out of the temple, with the
sheep and the oxen; and He poured out the coins of the
money changers and overturned their tables; and to
those who were selling the doves He said, 'Take these
things away; stop making My Father's house a place of
business.' His disciples remembered that it was written,
'Zeal for Your house will consume me.'" (2:13-17)

Following the Law, Jesus also went up to the temple to
celebrate the Passover. We say people went "up to the temple"
because Jerusalem is situated on a mountain 760 meters above
sea level. But when Jesus and His disciples arrived at the temple,
Jesus couldn't believe what He saw! The temple was crowded
with vendors trying to sell cattle, sheep, doves, etc., to the
people who had travelled from afar and had not been afforded
the opportunity to prepare anything to sacrifice to God.

People selling cattle, sheep, and doves were lined up, and
there were money changers sitting here and there exchanging
money for people because they said foreign money was unclean
to offer to God. The sound of people bargaining with each
other, and the cries of animals all mixed up together made such
a ruckus that the temple hardly seemed like a holy place of
worship.

Witnessing such a scene made Jesus' heart burn with fiery anger. So He made a whip out of cords and drove the animals out of the temple, He dumped the moneychangers' coins and overturned their tables. Then in a strict way He said to the people selling doves, "Take these things away; stop making My Father's house a place of business."

What do you think made Jesus, who is so gentle and never quarrelsome nor boisterous, so furious? He was not furious because He had a hot temper. He was furious because God's temple, a place that should be the most holy and clean place, was being tainted by vendors trying to make a profit for themselves. This scene shows us how much Jesus loved the temple.

One could ask, "Isn't it okay to buy and sell things that are needed for sacrifice to God?" However, the vendors were doing business for their own profit, and covering up God's glory. The temple is a place where we worship God in spirit and in truth, and a place where we offer up our prayers and praises to God. There should be no business transactions going on between and among believers in this place.

Even today, we must be careful not to do business in the church no matter the reason. Then one may ask, "But don't we sell books and other items in our church bookstore?" However, the purpose for running the bookstore in the church is not to earn a profit. The money raised from selling Bibles, Hymnals, and other items necessary for daily Christian life is used for helping the needy, to aid missions, and other programs for God's kingdom. Other than this, if anyone tries to do business in the church to earn personal profit, it should not be permitted.

In any place where people gather together in the Lord, we must make sure we don't bring into it the ways of the secular world. We can do this by doing everything in the truth. If with the slightest bit of fleshly thought we bring into the church the trends of the secular world, just as yeast rises and grows bigger, temptations and tribulations are sure to follow. Yes, God is loving and merciful; however, He will not tolerate actions that defile the church or cover up His glory.

The disciples who witnessed Jesus' rage then came to understand the Scripture, *"...Zeal for Your house will consume me"* (Psalm 69:9). The Pharisees, the Sadducees, and the teachers of the Law claimed to love God and therefore studied the laws and abided by them with zeal. They gathered at the temple to make sacrifices and to pray. But ultimately, they did not understand God's will. They appeared holy on the outside, but they were filled with evil and unrighteousness inside. They could not discern that the people were desecrating the temple by doing business therein.

In the same way, though the outward appearance of the temple is important, what's more important is our heart which, according to the Bible, is God's temple as well. God looks not at the outside of a man, but at the inner-most part of a man's heart. That is why in 1 Corinthians 3:16-17, it is written, *"Do you not know that you are a temple of God and that the Spirit of God dwells in you? If any man destroys the temple of God, God will destroy him, for the temple of God is holy, and that is what you are."*

Because the heart is where the Holy Spirit dwells, we must always abide by the Word, cast out evil, and strive to sanctify our hearts every day. Only when we do this can we correctly decipher God's will and live according to it.

"Destroy This Temple, and in Three Days I Will Raise it Up"

"The Jews then said to Him, 'What sign do You show us as your authority for doing these things?' Jesus answered them, 'Destroy this temple, and in three days I will raise it up.' The Jews then said, 'It took forty-six years to build this temple, and will You raise it up in three days?' But He was speaking of the temple of His body. So when He was raised from the dead, His disciples remembered that He said this; and they believed the Scripture and the word which Jesus had spoken." (2:18-22)

The vendors in the temple, the High Priest, the Sadducees, and the Pharisees were shocked to see Jesus overturning tables. People were asking, "What authority does He have to overturn something that the High Priest and Sadducees permitted?" If Jesus had the power and authority to do this, they wanted Him to prove it.

They asked, "What sign do You show us as your authority

for doing these things?" "Destroy this temple, and in three days I will raise it up," Jesus answered. The Jews who heard Jesus' reply laughed at Him. The temple in Jerusalem experienced as much suffering as the history of the nation of Israel itself. Built for the first time during King Solomon's reign, it was destroyed shortly after the invasion of King Nebuchadnezzar of Babylon. When the first group of people who were taken captive to Babylon from Judah returned home, they, along with Zerubbabel, rebuilt the temple for 20 years. But this temple was also destroyed by another invasion, and years later, King Herod, in order to gain the support of the people, rebuilt the temple for 46 years.

So we can see that building a temple is not an easy task. Building a temple requires a lot of resources and manpower, commitment and devotion. So when Jesus said He would rebuild the temple—which took 46 years to rebuild—in three days, of course the Jews thought He was being preposterous. We see later that they use this statement against Jesus when they convict Him (Matthew 26:61). On top of that, when Jesus was dying on the cross in order to fulfill God's salvation for mankind, they shouted, *"You who are going to destroy the temple and rebuild it in three days, save Yourself! If You are the Son of God, come down from the cross"* (Matthew 27:40; Mark 15:29-30).

When Jesus said, "in three days I will raise it up," He was saying that "I am the Lord of the temple." The spiritual meaning behind this statement is this: Jesus, who is the temple, will die on the cross and resurrect in three days.

If Jesus had said to them, "I am the Lord of the temple and the Son of the Creator God," they probably would have become enraged and retorted, "Who gave you the right to be the Lord of the temple?!" And if Jesus had said straightforwardly, "And though you will crucify Me on the cross because you hate Me, I will rise up again in three days," they would have become even more infuriated. That is why Jesus only made an indirect implication.

People of the flesh do not understand spiritual words. Even in the case of Jesus' disciples, they truly came to believe that Jesus is the Savior only *after* they witnessed Him dying on the cross and resurrecting again. And only *after* they received the Holy Spirit on the Pentecost did they become courageous witnesses of the gospel without fear for their lives. Therefore, one must have a spiritual experience *and* receive the Holy Spirit in order to truly understand God's Word and grow in faith.

"Now when He was in Jerusalem at the Passover, during the feast, many believed in His name, observing His signs which He was doing. But Jesus, on His part, was not entrusting Himself to them, for He knew all men, and because He did not need anyone to testify concerning man, for He Himself knew what was in man." (2:23-25)

For those people who wouldn't believe without signs and wonders, Jesus healed the sick and raised the dead. He showed them many powerful works. As a result, many people welcomed Him and wanted to invite Him to their homes. However, Jesus did not entrust Himself to them. This is because He knew the heart of men. What they wanted was not Jesus, but His power.

If Jesus didn't have any more power, their hearts would change. If something changes depending on the situation, it is not truth. However, those people who loved Jesus from the center of their hearts, brought joy to Jesus' heart. Mary and Martha, who lived in Bethany, were two such people. Because they truly loved Jesus from the center of their hearts, whenever He passed by that region, He visited their home (Luke 10:38).

Then what did Jesus mean when He said He did not need anyone to testify concerning man? This is because inside of a man's heart, there is envy, jealousy, murder, lust, and deceit. Jesus, who was without defect, righteous, and was only of the truth, did not want to be judged by them. These kinds of people cannot receive God's power, and they cannot give glory to God. To those people with true hearts, God will show them His power—to prove that He is with them—so that they may give Him glory.

Chapter 3

The Secret
to Being Born Again

The Conversation
with Nicodemus

While He was in Jerusalem at the Passover Feast, Jesus sanctified the temple, healed the sick, and preached messages that people had never heard before anywhere else. Many people saw the signs He was performing and came to believe in Him. One of these people was a Pharisee named Nicodemus, who was a member of the Jewish ruling council.

During Jesus' time, Judaism was mainly divided into the Pharisees, the Sadducees, and the Essenes. Of the three, the Pharisees believed in strict adherence to the laws, they believed in the resurrection of the dead, and they had the most power over the people. On the other hand the Sadducees looked down upon harsh adherence to the laws. They didn't believe in resurrection and eternal life and they denied the existence of angels and the spiritual realm. They were a denomination of realists. The Essenes focused more on achieving perfect harmony with God. They shared their possessions with one another, and they lived an ascetic life secluded from the rest of the world.

Nicodemus Seeks out Jesus

"Now there was a man of the Pharisees, named Nicodemus, a ruler of the Jews; this man came to Jesus by night and said to Him, 'Rabbi, we know that You have come from God as a teacher; for no one can do these signs that You do unless God is with him.'" (3:1-2)

The ruling council which Nicodemus was a member of was made up of 71 members including the high priest. The members of this council established and judged the laws, and they took on the roles equivalent to that of legislative and judicial branches of a government entity. This was possible because although Israel was under the rule of the Roman Empire, the Romans gave local authorities governing power over the people.

For he was an influential man of position and leadership, Nicodemus noticed that Jesus was not an ordinary person. Though he himself was a teacher, he felt there was unusual power in Jesus' teachings. And because Jesus was doing things like healing the sick and the crippled, which men cannot do, he acknowledged Him as someone sent from God.

: : A Public Meeting of the Sanhedrin (Model)

One night, he came to see Jesus. At that time, religious leaders like the Pharisees and the Sadducees accused Jesus by saying, "He is possessed by Beelzebub! By the prince of demons..." This was because many people were becoming followers of Jesus, and the Pharisees and Sadducees were afraid of losing their position and authority over the people.

But Nicodemus was different. He was always thirsty for the truth. Although he strictly abided by the laws, he was just not satisfied with that. At some point, he began to think that Jesus would be able to satiate his thirst for the truth. Though he came to see Jesus at night to avoid being seen by other people, he acknowledged Jesus as a good person, and wanted to know more about Him.

In the same way, everyone can hear about and witness the same power of God, but each person reacts differently. Upon witnessing God's power, some people are overjoyed and open their hearts very quickly. But some people don't even want to hear about such things and deny God's power entirely. Some evil people scavenge for any mishaps and try to find ways to create slander. The difference is the good and evil in each person's heart.

When Nicodemus met Jesus, he humbly lowered himself. Even though he himself was a man of position and leadership, he showed his respect to Jesus by calling Him "Rabbi", and confessing, "You have come from God as a teacher." Nicodemus said this because he knew that the miraculous signs Jesus was performing were not something just anyone could do, so he wanted to express his respect for Him.

The Meaning of Being "Born Again"

"Jesus answered and said to him, 'Truly, truly, I say to you, unless one is born again he cannot see the kingdom of God.' Nicodemus said to Him, 'How can a man be born when he is old? He cannot enter a second time into his mother's womb and be born, can he?'" (3:3-4)

After listening to Nicodemus' confession, Jesus makes an unexpected reply. When Nicodemus said to Him, "You have come from God as a teacher," Jesus doesn't say, "Yes, you're right." Instead, He says, "Truly, truly, I say to you, unless one is born again he cannot see the kingdom of God."

Just as Jesus saw the center of Nathanael's heart when Phillip first brought him to Jesus, Jesus also saw what was in the center of Nicodemus' heart. Nicodemus made such a confession because in his heart, he believed that Jesus was the Christ, and that He was God's Son. Because he had a good heart, seeing all the miraculous signs Jesus was performing, he simply thought that Jesus was a person of God. But this thought was not derived from spiritual enlightenment. That is why Jesus didn't say, "You're right," or "You're wrong." Instead, He teaches him a spiritual truth by telling him that he must be born again to see the kingdom of God.

What does it mean to be 'born again'? When someone who was always criticized by his or her neighbors turns over a new leaf and becomes a 'good' person, people often say "He's become a new person," or "She's been born again." But what Jesus is referring to here is not being born again in the physical nature, but being born again in the spiritual nature. Being born again in the spirit is when a person who used to live in the midst of untruth, listens to the Word of God and begins to live in the truth. For example, a person who used to be a liar changes into an honest person; or an angry and hateful person changes into a gentle and loving person.

There are times when people suffering from an incurable

disease meet God and are healed. They become so filled with God's grace and thanksgiving that their heart changes. But this doesn't mean they are immediately born again in the spirit. For this to happen, we need the help of the Holy Spirit. Only when we receive the Holy Spirit can we understand God's will, and only when we abide by God's will can we be born again in the spirit, and thereby receive eternal life.

Not understanding Jesus, Nicodemus asked how a person can be born twice. Of course he had to ask, since he couldn't understand. "How can a man be born when he is old? He cannot enter a second time into his mother's womb and be born, can he?"

A fetus grows in the mother's womb for nine months before being born into the world. Everyone knows that a person cannot go back into his mother's womb once he is born. Even though Nicodemus has thorough knowledge of the laws and he is a teacher of the laws, because he doesn't understand the spiritual message, he can't help but ask such a ridiculous question.

Being Born of Water and the Spirit

"Jesus answered, 'Truly, truly, I say to you, unless one is born of water and the Spirit he cannot enter into the kingdom of God.'" (3:5)

Nicodemus couldn't understand what Jesus meant by being 'born again', so when Jesus talked about being born of water and the Spirit, he just couldn't grasp what Jesus was talking about. Water quenches the thirst and works as a lubricant for all the organs in the body to function properly. Water maintains life, and it washes away all dirty things. So being "born of water" means to clean out all the dark and dirty things from the heart through God's Word.

Even though there is plenty of water before us, if we don't drink it, we cannot quench our thirst, and if we don't wash, we cannot become clean. The same goes for God's Word. Even if we know God's Word, if we don't abide by it, it is useless. So, as God tells us in the Bible, "Don't do this, cast off that," if we cast off hate, envy, jealousy, contempt, and condemnation, and other fruits of untruth from our hearts, then our hearts will become clean. Then, as God tells us, "Do this," or "Remember that;"we can become filled with love, sacrifice, the joy of benefitting others, and truths such as these in our hearts. Casting out untruth and becoming a person of truth by abiding in God's Word is being "born of water".

What then, does it mean to be "born of the Spirit"? Adam, the first ancestor of mankind, was a man created with a spirit, soul, and body (1 Thessalonians 5:23). But when he committed the sin of disobeying God by eating the fruit from the tree of the knowledge of good and evil, his spirit died. So from then on, man became a creature simply with a soul and body, just like animals (Ecclesiastes 3:18).

However, when we accept Jesus Christ as our Savior and receive the Holy Spirit, our spirit comes back to life and we become a child of God. In addition, our name is recorded in the

Book of Life in Heaven. The Holy Spirit dwells in our hearts and helps us realize that we are sinners and leads us to repent. The Holy Spirit also gives us the grace, strength, and power to live according to God's Word.

Even though we may know much about God's Word, we cannot act according to it without the help of the Holy Spirit. If God's word remains as mere knowledge in our heads, then salvation cannot be received through it. After we plant a seed, we need to nourish it and take care of it until we see its fruit. Likewise, after we receive the Holy Spirit, we need the Holy Spirit's help to nourish and take care of our spirit so it can grow and mature. So being born of the Spirit means abiding by God's Word with the help of the Holy Spirit, and becoming a person of truth—a person who resembles the image of God. When this happens, we receive salvation and can enter into Heaven.

If we have God's Word but not the Holy Spirit, we cannot have victory over the world or the enemy devil. Even if the Holy Spirit comes to us, if we don't have God's Word, we cannot be cleansed. God's Word and the Holy Spirit work together to lead us to Heaven. That is why we need to be "born of water and the Spirit".

A Person Born of the Holy Spirit

"That which is born of the flesh is flesh, and that which is born of the Spirit is spirit. Do not be amazed that I said to you, 'You must be born again.' The wind

blows where it wishes and you hear the sound of it, but do not know where it comes from and where it is going; so is everyone who is born of the Spirit." (3:6-8)

Nicodemus was puzzled by what Jesus said, but he tried to receive it with a good heart. Because Jesus knew his heart, He continued to talk to him. If Nicodemus was like the other Pharisees and Sadducees, who would try to find a point of argument anywhere they could, then Jesus probably would have stopped talking with him.

Nicodemus becomes even more befuddled when Jesus begins talking about "the flesh" and "the spirit." "The flesh" literally means "the skin" or "the body." But the spiritual definition of "the flesh" is anything that perishes or changes; anything that is not eternal. "The flesh" signifies all perishable things such as: everything under the sun, hate, envy, jealousy, adultery, dissension—anything that is not of God and not of the truth.

So why does Jesus say, "Flesh gives birth to flesh"? In order to understand this, we must first know the characteristics of mud, or soil. Depending on what it is mixed with, the quality of the soil changes. One of the qualities of soil is that it decomposes and changes; therefore soil is of the 'flesh'.

Because man was created from dust, or soil, his original nature is of the 'flesh'. When God created the first man, man was made of fertile soil. Then God blew the breath of life into man's nostrils and man became a living being with a living spirit. Yes, Adam, the first man had a spirit, but he was not a perfect being like God. Man was not a living spirit by himself;

he became a living spirit because God blew His power into him. And, because man was not perfect, with his free will he ate the forbidden fruit. As a result, Adam's spirit died, and he returned to being simply a man of flesh.

And to this man, who returned to just being of the flesh, or a perishable being, the enemy devil and Satan planted all kinds of untruths into him. This is why not even one generation after Adam's family was banned from the Garden of Eden, the first case of murder occurred—and that was committed by a brother against his own brother.

Adam's two sons, Cain and Abel both made sacrifices to God, but God only accepted Abel's sacrifice, because it was a proper sacrifice. Cain became jealous and killed Abel. Because Adam became a man of flesh, his descendants also were of the flesh, and so with each succeeding generation, man became more and more evil. Eventually, all of man's thoughts and desires became things of untruth, and things of the flesh, which ultimately perish and change. This is what Jesus meant when He said, "Flesh gives birth to flesh."

Therefore people who are like this, who are simply of the flesh, cannot enter into Heaven, which is in the spiritual realm. That is why in 1 Corinthians 15:50 it says, *"...flesh and blood cannot inherit the kingdom of God, nor does the perishable inherit the imperishable."* How then, can a man of flesh enter into God's kingdom? "The Spirit must give birth to spirit". The spirit is totally opposite of the flesh. The spirit does not perish or change; it is eternal. Only the Holy Spirit can give birth to spirit.

As explained before, the Holy Spirit revives our spirit, which was once dead; and not only that, it continually matures our spirit. The Holy Spirit helps us spot our sins and constantly tries to revive the "good" in our hearts. The Holy Spirit tells us, "Don't go to the way of eternal condemnation. This is sin, and it is untruth. This way is the way of righteousness." When we try to live in the truth, by the help of the Holy Spirit, the "flesh" begins to peel away from us. For example, God's Word tells us, "Do not hate." If we try to obey this word by pushing hate out of our hearts, love, which is the opposite of the untruth of hate, takes place in our hearts. This is the case where "the Spirit gives birth to spirit."

When Jesus tried to explain by making a distinction between the fleshly world and the spiritual world, Nicodemus couldn't grasp what He was talking about. This is because the spiritual world is not something you can understand with worldly knowledge. Only with the help of the Holy Spirit can one understand it. Though Nicodemus was scholarly and very knowledgeable, he was ignorant about the spiritual world, so he could not understand Jesus. So to help him understand better, Jesus explains again using "wind" as an illustration.

When we see leaves shaking, we can tell that the wind is blowing, but we cannot tell when and where the wind came from. Just as we don't know the course of the wind, a person of the flesh cannot fully understand a person born of the Spirit. Since a person born of the Spirit distances himself from worldly pleasures and lives a very self-controlled, temperate life, people of the flesh might ask, "What does that person do for fun?" But a person born of water and the Spirit lives according to God's

Word, so he is filled with the true peace and joy that comes from the hope of Heaven that God gives to him.

Nicodemus Asks Yet Again

"Nicodemus said to Him, 'How can these things be?' Jesus answered and said to him, 'Are you the teacher of Israel and do not understand these things? Truly, truly, I say to you, we speak of what we know and testify of what we have seen, and you do not accept our testimony.'" (3:9-11)

Even after Jesus explained using the wind illustration, Nicodemus still didn't understand. So he asked again. By this we can see his earnest desire to learn about the spiritual world. He asked, "How can these things be?"

At this question, Jesus replies with a question, "Are you the teacher of Israel and do not understand these things?" Jesus didn't ask this question to belittle Nicodemus or ridicule him. He just truly wanted Nicodemus to understand, since he knew God, and he was a teacher of the laws, but still he didn't understand the spiritual world. In reality, at the time Nicodemus came to visit Jesus, Jesus had already been in ministry for some time. Therefore Nicodemus had already known about, and had heard Jesus' testimony about what He saw regarding Heaven. He also knew about all the signs and wonders Jesus had performed. But he still couldn't understand. That's why he was continuing to ask.

At the time, though many people saw the signs and wonders Jesus performed, they still couldn't believe. The reason why they couldn't believe was not because they had no knowledge about the spiritual world, but it was because their hearts were evil and calloused. Either they were spiritually arrogant, or they thought that what they saw didn't coincide with the knowledge of the laws they set up for themselves. So, they ended up criticizing and judging Jesus' teachings and wonders. In order to help these people understand, Jesus talked about "what we know," which would be God's truth, or His Word, and He testified about "what we have seen," which would be the spiritual world, signs, and wonders. But Jesus stated that people still do not listen nor do they believe.

The "people" whom Jesus talked about included Nicodemus. This is because his spiritual eyes weren't opened yet, and he was in a situation where he didn't understand the spiritual things yet either. However, Nicodemus did not come to Jesus with an evil heart, so ultimately, he ended up accepting the Lord, and his whole life changed as a result. Later on, even though he wasn't in the situation to support Jesus, he still defended Him, and after Jesus' death on the cross, Nicodemus even brought the spices to use on Jesus' body (John 7:51, 19:39-40).

"If I told you earthly things and you do not believe, how will you believe if I tell you heavenly things? No one has ascended into heaven, but He who descended from heaven: the Son of Man." (3:12-13)

When Jesus taught the Word of God, He used many

allegories, such as talents, the soil, the vineyard, etc. This is because it is not easy to clearly describe the spiritual world with the language of this world. But even if that were possible, Jesus knew that people still wouldn't believe. Like them, Nicodemus also couldn't understand, even after listening to several illustrations on several occasions. So how could Jesus talk to him about heavenly things?

"He who descended from heaven" is Jesus. Every person is conceived and born through the union of their parents' sperm and egg. But Jesus was conceived by the Holy Spirit, so He is called "the one who descended from heaven". In the Bible it says that before Jesus, Enoch and Elijah went up to Heaven without dying. But why does it also say, "No one has ascended into heaven, but He who descended from heaven: the Son of Man," speaking of Jesus?

Enoch and Elijah are Adam's descendants, just like us. Therefore they were born with original sin. Although they did not commit sins during their lifetime here on earth, they still had the original sin they inherited from their parents. Then how did they ascend into Heaven without dying? Enoch and Elijah lived during the Old Testament times. This was before Jesus came, and before the Holy Spirit came as the Helper. However, with faith, they overcame their original sin. They took control over and overcame the original sin within their hearts with faith, and so became free from the spiritual law which states, "For the wages of sin is death." By this we can see how great their faith was.

Jesus, on the other hand, who was conceived by the Holy Spirit had no sin whatsoever from the very beginning. Jesus came into this world to die on the cross to save us from our sins; He then resurrected, and ascended into Heaven, all according to God's providence. So what this passage means is that aside from Jesus, there was no one else who went up to Heaven without any original sin or committed sins.

Prophecy of Jesus' Death on the Cross

"As Moses lifted up the serpent in the wilderness, even so must the Son of Man be lifted up; so that whoever believes will in Him have eternal life." (3:14-15)

Once again, Jesus used the story of the Israelites' exodus out of Egypt to help Nicodemus understand. The Israelites that followed Moses out of Egypt saw God's power. They experienced all kinds of miraculous events, such as the ten plagues on Egypt, the dividing of the Red Sea, and the bitter water of Marah turning into sweet water. But each time they faced a hardship, they failed to show their faith. Instead, they held resentment against God, as if they never experienced His power.

Even though God freed them from 400 years of harsh slavery, they totally forgot about this grace and complained that He was making them 'die in the desert'. They even called manna, which God gave them to eat, "miserable food", and regarded God's blessing with contempt (Numbers 21:5). And they insisted that even if they had to live as slaves again, they would be better off dying in Egypt. As a result, God turned His face away from them, and venomous snakes came and bit them.

Only on the verge of death did they regret their actions and finally repent.

When Moses prayed on their behalf, God told him how the Israelites could be saved from death. Moses was told to make a bronze snake and put it on a pole, and then tell those who were bitten by snakes to look at the bronze snake to live. Even if they just had such small faith to simply obey Moses and look at the bronze snake, God wanted to acknowledge that as faith, and save their lives.

Spiritually, a snake represents the enemy devil and Satan, and it is also a symbol for death. Because the serpent tempted Eve and made all of mankind go the way of death, he is the incarnation of sin. So why would God tell Moses to make a snake, which symbolizes sin and death, and have him put it on a pole?

This foreshadows God's providence of salvation: the death of Jesus Christ upon the cross. Jesus would be taking up all of mankind's sins and dying on the cross. That is why God made Moses create the snake, which represents sin and death, and had him put it on a pole. Just like everyone who looked at the bronze snake on the pole was saved from death, everyone who believes in the salvation by the cross is saved from eternal death and gains eternal life.

Sometimes people ask, "Since Moses made a bronze image and had people look at it, isn't this considered idol worship?" If you don't understand the spiritual meaning of God's Word and His providence, you can have this kind of misconception. However, this event was only a way to foreshadow God's plan of salvation by Jesus' death on the cross to pay for the penalty of man's sins. It was in no way for the purpose of worshipping the bronze snake.

The Love of God Who Gave His Only Begotten Son

"For God so loved the world, that He gave His only begotten Son, that whoever believes in Him shall not perish, but have eternal life. For God did not send the Son into the world to judge the world, but that the world might be saved through Him." (3:16-17)

In many parts of the Bible, it says, *"Do not love the world"* (1 John 2:15), but in this verse, it says that God loved the world. What does this mean? When the Bible says "Do not love the world", it means don't love anything that goes against God's will, such as lawlessness, untruth, and a life of sin. It means do not sin or live in darkness, but live by God's Word and live in the Light. When the Bible says, "God loved the world", it means that God loves people, and everything related to them.

God, who planned for the cultivation of mankind in order to share His love with them, created the natural world and everything in this world that man needs to live. Just like new parents who joyfully prepare everything for their newborn child, God joyfully prepared everything in creation to prepare for man, who would be created in His image. Because God loved people so much, He loved everything that He created for them as well. Eventually, when people sinned and had to go the way of death, God sent His only begotten Son, Jesus, to save them from eternal death.

There are some people who misconceive God as only a scary God of judgment. However, it clearly says in verse 17 that God did not send Jesus to condemn the world, but to save it.

Faith and Eternal Life

"He who believes in Him is not judged; he who does not believe has been judged already, because he has not believed in the name of the only begotten Son of God. This is the judgment, that the Light has come into the world, and men loved the darkness rather than the Light, for their deeds were evil. For everyone who does evil hates the Light, and does not come to the Light for fear that his deeds will be exposed. But he who practices the truth comes to the Light, so that his deeds may be manifested as having been wrought in God." (3:18-21)

Acts 4:12 says, *"And there is salvation in no one else; for there is no other name under heaven that has been given among men by which we must be saved."* Even if a person is hailed as a saint, or makes great achievements for society, he or she cannot save us. The only way to be saved is to receive Jesus Christ with faith. Faith here does not simply mean knowing in our heads how to be saved. Faith means trying to become more like Christ by living according to God's Word, casting out untruth, and becoming a person of truth.

Then why does the Scripture say that those who don't accept Jesus Christ as their Savior stand condemned already? This is because there is no other name than Jesus Christ through whom salvation can be received, and those who do not believe in Him do not live in the Light and do not live according to the truth, and so they cannot be saved. If someone who hasn't received Jesus Christ dies right now, he has to go to Hell. That is why the Scripture says these people stand condemned already.

While sharing the gospel, we occasionally meet people who either dislike Christians or feel sorry for them. They love darkness more than the Light, and they don't know the joy and thanksgiving of receiving the Holy Spirit, and the hope of Heaven, so they think being a Christian is boring.

Seeing through the heart of these people, Jesus said, "For everyone who does evil hates the Light, and does not come to the Light for fear that his deeds will be exposed." On the contrary, people who follow the truth, who accepted the Lord and received the Holy Spirit, try to conduct a life that's focused on glorifying God. They do this because they know that through God, all of their problems can be solved, all of their blessings come from Him, and they will eventually go to Heaven.

The One Who Descends
from Heaven

Where there is water, people gather and villages form. Likewise, people who are yearning and thirsty for righteousness gather where there is God's Word, which is the water of life. When Jesus, who was Himself the Word, began spreading the gospel about Heaven and began baptizing, many people naturally gathered around Him. This was because just as the recorder of Psalms confessed, *"How sweet are Your words to my taste! Yes, sweeter than honey to my mouth!"* (Psalm 119:103), the Word of God was sweet.

"After these things Jesus and His disciples came into the land of Judea, and there He was spending time with them and baptizing. John also was baptizing in Aenon near Salim, because there was much water there; and

people were coming and were being baptized—for John had not yet been thrown into prison. Therefore there arose a discussion on the part of John's disciples with a Jew about purification. And they came to John and said to him, 'Rabbi, He who was with you beyond the Jordan, to whom you have testified, behold, He is baptizing and all are coming to Him.'" (3:22-26)

While Jesus was baptizing, John the Baptist was also baptizing at Aenon, near the western side of the Jordan, where there was plenty of water. Many of John's followers began following Jesus. Seeing this, other disciples of John the Baptist became uneasy.

Up to this point, many people looked up to John the Baptist as a great prophet and followed him. They were proud of being his disciples. But the situation changed, and more people were gathering around Jesus, whom their teacher had baptized, so they reported this to John in a disgruntled way.

"Rabbi, He who was with you beyond the Jordan, to whom you have testified, behold, He is baptizing and all are coming to Him."

"He must increase; I must decrease."

"John answered and said, 'A man can receive nothing unless it has been given him from heaven. You yourselves are my witnesses that I said, "I am not the Christ," but, "I have been sent ahead of Him." He who has the bride is the bridegroom; but the friend of the bridegroom, who stands and hears him, rejoices greatly because of the bridegroom's voice. So this joy of mine has been made full. He must increase, but I must decrease.'" (3:27-30)

John's disciples thought John would understand their troubled hearts, but John's reaction was totally different. John testifies that because it is God's will, it is only right that people follow Jesus. He taught his disciples the truth.

If we apply this situation to today's time, what would that be like? Let's say there were people who were searching here and there because they were thirsty for God's Word. If their pastor worries that they might go to another church and begin to talk negatively about the church and the pastor, then his heart would be very far from John's heart. Or, if we hear someone talking negatively about another person and our ears perk up, we are no different from John's disciples. Even if we hear a person saying negative things about another person, we should not join in; rather, we should enlighten those involved in the negative conversation with the truth, and cast away the darkness from that situation.

Because John the Baptist knew God's will, he was able to tell his disciples what *his* calling is, and what *their* calling is. And to make sure his disciples don't become disappointed, he uses an illustration to tell them who Jesus is. The main person at a wedding who awaits the bride is the bridegroom. So the friends of the bridegroom share the joy and bless the groom.

John is trying to explain that since Jesus, the bridegroom has come, as the bridegroom's friend, John's joy is overflowing. Although he baptized Jesus, John knew that Jesus would be the one saving his people from sin, and that Jesus was the one with great power. That is why it brought him more joy to rather lift Jesus higher and serve Him.

Most people become uncomfortable when others are more successful than they are at something, or in some situation. But John was different. He didn't mind whatever came of himself; he only hoped that everything would go well with Jesus. He lowers himself by saying, "He must increase, but I must decrease." John's heart was the kind of heart that was just joyful even if another person was more loved and more recognized than him.

The Testimony of the One from Above

"He who comes from above is above all, he who is of the earth is from the earth and speaks of the earth. He who comes from heaven is above all. What He has seen and heard, of that He testifies; and no one receives His testimony. He who has received His testimony has set his seal to this, that God is true." (3:31-33)

John the Baptist knew that Jesus was one who came from above. John testified that as the one who created the universe, Jesus is the King of kings, Lord of lords, and that He is above all. John also says that one who "is of the earth" is from the earth and speaks like one from the earth. Then where do we belong? Since we received Jesus Christ, and were saved through faith, we have become children of God, and citizens of Heaven, therefore we belong to Heaven.

Of course, even if we believe in Jesus, if we have not received the Holy Spirit yet, we are still people of the flesh, and still "one of the earth". A person who "belongs to the earth" hears God's Word, but cannot believe in it. It was the same in Jesus' time. Jesus testified about what He has seen and heard in Heaven, but people didn't believe Him. They rather persecuted Him and tried to kill Him.

But those with a good heart accept His testimony and His Words. When they open their heart and accept Jesus Christ, God gives them the Holy Spirit as a gift, and they gain the right to become a child of God. So the Creator God becomes their Father and they receive the assurance that they belong to Heaven. Then, they can confess that God is the truth, and they obey His Words.

Eternal Life and God's Wrath

"For He whom God has sent speaks the words of God; for He gives the Spirit without measure. The Father loves the Son and has given all things into His hand. He who believes in the Son has eternal life; but he who does not obey the Son will not see life, but the wrath of God abides on him." (3:34-36)

Jesus, whom God sent, only spoke the Words of God. Only God's Word is true and eternal. God gave Him the Spirit without measure, so He spoke the Words of God in the fullness of the Holy Spirit.

The same word applies to us today. To those who received the testimony, to those who believe that God is true, God gives them the Spirit without measure. So those who accepted Jesus Christ as their Savior and are overflowing with God's grace testify about God and Jesus Christ in the fullness of the Holy Spirit.

Because the Father God loved the Son, He placed everything in Jesus' hands. Jesus was blameless and pure, and He was God Himself; however, He took on the body of a servant and came to this earth and obeyed even to the point of death. So how could God not love Him? Because He loved Him that much, God placed everything in His hands.

People who believe in this Son obey His Words and act in the truth. So life is in them, and they walk toward eternal life. But those who don't obey the Son cannot see eternal life, and instead God's wrath abides on them. The Scripture says the wrath of God 'abides on' them because God's wrath could leave or remain according to whether or not they repent and obey while living a disobedient life. That is why the Scripture is saying, "he who does not obey the Son will not see life, but the wrath of God abides on him." But if these people repent and turn back to God, He will forgive them and love them.

Chapter 4

Jesus' Method of Evangelism

1. Jesus' Conversation with the Samaritan Woman
(4:1-26)

2. Jesus Teaches His Disciples
(4:27-42)

3. The Second Sign in Cana
(4:43-54)

Jesus' Conversation
with the Samaritan Woman

Who you meet and *when* you meet them can define a major turning point in your life. In John chapter 4, we can see how one Samaritan woman's life totally changed after meeting Jesus.

In Jewish society, religious leaders like the Pharisees and teachers of the law were not pleased about Jesus preaching to the people. All they did was to look for the opportune moment to trap Jesus in a snare any way they could. At about that time, they began to hear about Jesus baptizing more people than John.

Jesus Passes by Samaria

"Therefore when the Lord knew that the Pharisees had heard that Jesus was making and baptizing more

disciples than John (although Jesus Himself was not baptizing, but His disciples were), He left Judea and went away again into Galilee. And He had to pass through Samaria." (4:1-4)

Even though Jesus wasn't the one baptizing, rumors told otherwise. It was Jesus' disciples baptizing, but people still came to be baptized. Then the Pharisees began to grow jealous, and questioned, "Who is this Jesus that baptizes?" Knowing what was going on in the hearts of the Pharisees, Jesus left Judea and returned to Galilee to avoid a confrontation with them.

There are two ways to get from Judea to Galilee. One is a straight route starting from Jerusalem through the region of Samaria. The second route is starting from Jerusalem and travelling northbound along the Jordan River, which is the longer and more rugged route. However, the Jews most often took the second route. They had their reasons.

Essentially, Samaritans are also descendants of Abraham. In 722 B.C., after the Assyrians captured Northern Israel, they took many people as captives, and moved many foreigners into that region. At this time, the Israelites who were left in Samaria intermarried with the foreigners and lost the pure bloodline of Israel. So a Samaritan was a mixed person born from one Israelite and one non-Israelite parent.

On the other hand, when Southern Judah was captured by Babylon, the Jews there were also relocated by force, but they did not mix with other races. And during Nehemiah's time, the Jews who returned to their homeland of Judea began an extensive project to reclaim their heritage. In the case that a Jew had intermarried with a foreign woman and had a child, they made the foreign woman and the child return to the woman's homeland, so that only the pure bloodline of Jacob remained. This is how strong the Jewish people's ethnic pride was, and as a result, they treated Samaritans like dogs and did not like to associate with them.

And after the Jews repatriated and were in the process of rebuilding their temple in Jerusalem, the Samaritans constantly interfered and hindered the Jews' reconstruction project so much that the two nations became enemies. So the Jews even considered stepping on the Samaritans' land as despicable, and when travelling from Judea to Galilee, they preferred to go the long route around Samaria. However, Jesus, who only had love and no evil in His heart, decided to go through the land of Samaria.

The Samaritan Woman Who Met Jesus

"So He came to a city of Samaria called Sychar, near the parcel of ground that Jacob gave to his son Joseph; and Jacob's well was there. So Jesus, being wearied from His journey, was sitting thus by the well. It was about the sixth hour. There came a woman of Samaria to draw water. Jesus said to her, 'Give Me a drink.' For His disciples had gone away into the city to buy food. Therefore the Samaritan woman said to Him, 'How is it that You, being a Jew, ask me for a drink since I am a Samaritan woman?' (For Jews have no dealings with

Samaritans.)" (4:5-9)

While Jesus was passing through Samaria, He came to a town called "Sychar". Jacob's well was there (the well that Jacob dug for his son Joseph). You may think, "What's so special about a small well that it's commemorated with a name?" However, in the span of one year, between April and October, Israel receives close to no rain. Therefore water is very important to this nation. So wells are very valuable in Israel.

It is written that Jesus sat by the well because He was tired from the journey, but this was recorded from the perspective of His disciples. Because they themselves were tired, they assumed Jesus was tired too.

While Jesus was resting, the disciples went into town to buy some food. About this time, there was a Samaritan woman who came to the well to draw some water. She could have come out at a different time to avoid the sun at its strongest, but the woman chose to come to the well at this time. Being midday, the woman didn't expect to see many people. Then, she saw a stranger resting by the well. He was most assuredly a Jew, so she wondered why he was passing through Samaria.

Jesus asked the woman for a drink. The woman was shocked. She was shocked, because when a Jew looks at a Samaritan, he usually acts as if he's seen a bug. Simply put, Jews never associate with Samaritans. But this one was talking to her! In actuality, Jesus travelling through Samaria to get to Galilee was according to God's will—for the purpose of spreading the gospel in Samaria. The disciples going into town, and the woman coming to the well at that very moment was not by chance. Everything

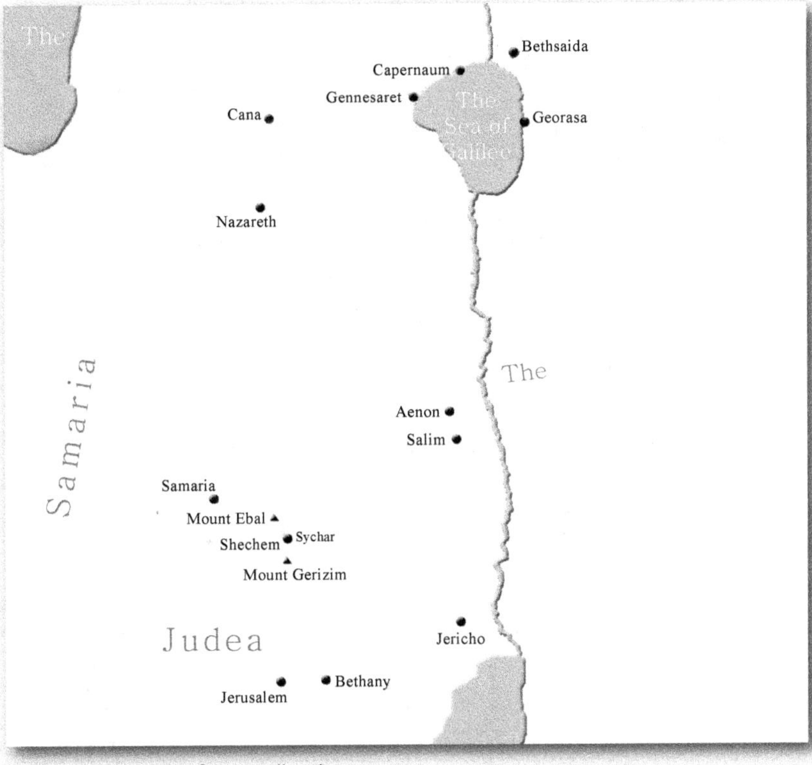

The

Bethsaida

Capernaum

Gennesaret

The
Sea of
Galilee

Cana

Georasa

Nazareth

The

Samaria

Aenon

Salim

Samaria

Mount Ebal ▲

Shechem ● Sychar

Mount Gerizim ▲

Judea

Jericho

Jerusalem

● Bethany

:: Samaria and the Surrounding Areas

:: Jacob's Well, located at the foot of Mount Ebal in Northern Shechem

was orchestrated by God.

"You Are Not Greater than our Father Jacob, Are You?"

"Jesus answered and said to her, 'If you knew the gift of God, and who it is who says to you, "Give Me a drink," you would have asked Him, and He would have given you living water.' She said to Him, 'Sir, You have nothing to draw with and the well is deep; where then do You get that living water? You are not greater than our father Jacob, are You, who gave us the well, and drank of it himself and his sons and his cattle?'" (4:10-12)

To the woman who cannot hide her astonishment, Jesus shares about God's gift, and Himself. Here, "God's gift" signifies the Holy Spirit. As it is written in Acts 2:38, *"Repent, and each of you be baptized in the name of Jesus Christ for the forgiveness of your sins; and you will receive the gift of the Holy Spirit."*

Jesus is explaining that if she knew that the one asking for water was the Savior, she would ask Him for the Holy Spirit and the living water. But since she does not know, she is not asking. So Jesus tries to teach her that truth. But not understanding the deeper meaning of what He is talking about, she responds after perceiving only the physical situation at hand, asking, "Sir, You have nothing to draw with and the well is deep; where then do You get that living water?" Jesus is talking about the Holy Spirit and the water of eternal life. But the woman does not understand the spiritual meaning behind His words, so she ends up asking such a question. She is similar to Nicodemus, who didn't understand the spiritual meaning of being "born again".

Then all of a sudden, the woman asks if Jesus is greater than Jacob. Since Jesus said He could give her living water, she was comparing Him to her ancestor, Jacob, who gave his people the well to draw water from. This was because the woman considered her ancestor Jacob as a great person. If she knew that the person before her eyes was the Savior, she would have responded differently.

The Water I Give is the Water of Eternal Life

"Jesus answered and said to her, 'Everyone who drinks of this water will thirst again; but whoever drinks of the water that I will give him shall never thirst; but the water that I will give him will become in him a well of water springing up to eternal life.' The woman said to Him, 'Sir, give me this water, so I will not be thirsty nor come all the way here to draw.'" (4:13-15)

Water is an essential element for life. The woman always came to the well to draw water, but after drinking the water, her thirst was satiated only for a short time, and a little bit later, her thirst would come back. But since Jesus says He could give her water that would let her never thirst again, what wonderful news! Jesus enlightens the woman on the most important factor of life, and thereby helps her to open her heart.

Only then does the woman realize that the water Jesus is talking about is different from the water she is thinking about. Because Jesus said, "but whoever drinks of the water that I will give him shall never thirst," the woman thought, "Oh, he must be talking about something different here." The one giving her this message appeared true to her, so she had this thought in her heart, "I don't fully understand, but I better learn from him and believe what he says." So she said to Jesus, "Sir, give me this water, so I will not be thirsty nor come all the way here to draw."

> **"He said to her, 'Go, call your husband and come here.' The woman answered and said, 'I have no husband.' Jesus said to her, 'You have correctly said, "I have no husband"; for you have had five husbands, and the one whom you now have is not your husband; this you have said truly.'" (4:16-18)**

The woman is asking Jesus for the water of eternal life. But Jesus doesn't give her the water He offered. Instead, he tells her to call her husband. This was very strange to the woman. She said, "I have no husband."

Then Jesus speaks as if He already knew everything, and says she had five husbands. The fact that a total stranger knew her past so well shocked her even more. As Jesus said, the woman had five husbands. After all the turbulence in her life, she met the man she was currently with, but this man also could not offer her true love and joy.

So this woman knew very well that she cannot expect to receive that kind of love from any person. Therefore she was waiting for the Christ, whom the prophecies of Old Testament had told her about—the true groom who would save her and be with her for eternity. And because she hadn't met this Messiah yet, she confessed that she had no husband. Seeing her heart, Jesus acknowledges her words. "You have correctly said, 'I have no husband.'"

Instead of rebuking her by saying, "Why do you lie? The man you're living with now, isn't he your husband?" He takes her word for it and accepts it. And when Jesus tells her, "Go, call your husband and come here," He's not trying to dig up her past. He was trying to solve the most important problem in her life. And because He knew her heart and her circumstances very well, He says, "... this you have said truly."

"I Perceive that You Are a Prophet"

"The woman said to Him, 'Sir, I perceive that You are a prophet. Our fathers worshiped in this mountain, and you people say that in Jerusalem is the place where men ought to worship.'" (4:19-20)

Since a stranger that she had never met, and never talked to before, knew her heart and her circumstances so well, she was shaking from astonishment. And she knew this was no ordinary man she was talking to. She was quite sure that He was a prophet that she had learned about from other people, or her ancestors.

So when she called Jesus "Sir", she was trying to show Him her respect though she could not possibly have imagined that the person in front of her was the Messiah. But, simply perceiving Him as a prophet, she asks Him about something she has always been curious about, a question about the place of worship.

At this time, Jews worshipped at the temple in Jerusalem, but the Samaritans worshipped at a temple on top of Mount Gerizim, within their land. During King Rehoboam's reign, Israel was divided into Northern and Southern Kingdoms. And Jeroboam, the king of Northern Israel built shrines on the high places in order to prevent people from going to Jerusalem. Having vaguely heard about these historical facts, she was curious to know where the proper place to worship was.

"Woman, Believe Me"

> **"Jesus said to her, 'Woman, believe Me, an hour is coming when neither in this mountain nor in Jerusalem will you worship the Father. You worship what you do not know; we worship what we know, for salvation is from the Jews." (4:21-22)**

To the people of Israel, the place of worship has significant meaning. The temple is where God's presence is, so it is set apart as holy. The Jews believed that the temple was the center of the universe. However, more significant than the place of worship, is how we worship—with what kind of heart we worship. God is pleased when people act in goodness and worship God with a true love for God, but He does not accept the worship of those people who worship with evil in their hearts.

The Samaritan woman didn't have accurate knowledge about God and the Messiah, so she wasn't able to give proper worship. Samaria had lost its cultural identity and became a polytheistic society where idol worship was prevalent, so the woman didn't know about God very accurately. If she had accurate information about God and the Messiah, she probably would have recognized that the man in front of her was the Messiah.

People who truly revered God quickly recognized Jesus as the Messiah. They also knew—just as the prophets of old had prophesied—that salvation would come from the line of David; someone born in Bethlehem, in the land of Judea. This is why Jesus said to the woman, "You worship what you do not know; we worship what we know, for salvation is from the Jews."

"An Hour Is Coming When the True Worshipers Will Worship God in Spirit and in Truth"

"But an hour is coming, and now is, when the true worshipers will worship the Father in spirit and truth; for such people the Father seeks to be His worshipers. God is spirit, and those who worship Him must worship in spirit and truth." (4:23-24)

Worship is the formality in which we give reverence and

adoration to God. It is giving praises and glory to God and thereby lifting up His holy name. The reason why man should worship God is because God created the universe for man, and He also sent His only begotten Son, Jesus Christ, to save him from sin.

However, God does not receive just any kind of worship. We can see this through Cain and Abel's worship. Abel made a sacrifice to God using the first born lamb and fat, and Cain made a sacrifice using the crops of the field. Cain worshipped God in the flesh, according to what he thought was the correct form of worship. Abel, on the other hand, worshipped God in spirit, according to God's will, using sacrificial blood. God accepted only Abel's worship.

So what does it mean to worship in spirit? What is the kind of worship that God accepts? It is offering worship to God in spirit and in truth. Worshipping in spirit means to take in the 66 books of the Bible as nourishment according to the guidance of the Holy Spirit, and worshipping from the center of one's heart. Worshipping in truth means to worship with all of our body, mind, will, and sincerity; with joy, thanksgiving, prayer, praise, deeds, and offerings. When we worship God in this way, God will accept our worship and protect us from accidents, illnesses, and dangers. He will also bless our businesses and workplaces.

Jesus answered the Samaritan woman with an answer she was not expecting, talking about spiritual worship. He spoke of an hour that is coming when we will worship in spirit and in truth. This "hour" that Jesus mentioned refers to the time after

Jesus' resurrection and ascension into Heaven which is from the moment the Holy Spirit comes, until Jesus' return in the air. But the woman could not totally understand what it meant to worship in spirit and in truth.

"I Who Speak to You Am He"

"The woman said to Him, 'I know that Messiah is coming (He who is called Christ); when that One comes, He will declare all things to us.' Jesus said to her, 'I who speak to you am He.'" (4:25-26)

The Samaritan woman was earnestly waiting for the Messiah that her ancestors and prophets of Old Testament had spoken about. But she didn't know who He was. Even the Jews, who claimed to know the laws didn't think that the Messiah would be the Savior of the world; they simply thought he was going to be some king who would save them from the oppression of the Roman Empire.

Jesus tells her a secret that totally takes her by surprise. That He Himself was the Messiah. "I who speak to you am He."

With layers of pain and suffering buried in her heart, this woman was waiting solely for this Messiah. Now that He was standing before her very eyes, how thrilled she must have been! Like a fog that vanishes into thin air, all her doubts vanished away in that instant. Without even a hint of doubt, she believed Jesus' words.

Jesus Teaches His Disciples

How much time passed by? While Jesus was sharing the gospel with the Samaritan woman, His disciples returned after buying some food. They knew that Jesus knew no one in Samaria. However, they saw Him talking with a woman as if He had known her for a very long time.

> **"At this point His disciples came, and they were amazed that He had been speaking with a woman, yet no one said, 'What do You seek?' or, 'Why do You speak with her?'" (4:27)**

All the disciples thought it was strange that Jesus was talking to a Samaritan woman, but no one asked Him forthright what He was doing. Because they knew from watching Jesus on a daily basis that His words and His actions were always of the truth, and that in Him there was no deceit or untruth. Therefore none of them could easily say that what He was doing was "right" or "wrong". Jews don't associate with Samaritans, but they knew that if Jesus was talking to a Samaritan woman, there had to be a special reason. That is why they didn't question Him.

However, if the disciples had no heart to judge or condemn from the very beginning, they probably wouldn't have been "surprised" in the first place. Every person decides what is right or wrong according to his own knowledge, education, experience, and wisdom. When something doesn't coincide with his personal thoughts, he easily judges and condemns. But one's knowledge, theory, or experience is not always the truth, so one's judgment can always be wrong.

The Samaritan Woman Evangelizes

"So the woman left her waterpot, and went into the city and said to the men, 'Come, see a man who told me all the things that I have done; this is not the Christ, is it?' They went out of the city, and were coming to Him." (4:28-30)

Because of the joy of meeting the Messiah, she forgot why she was at the well, and leaving her waterpot, she rushed into town. Why did she not need the waterpot anymore? Now that she's met Jesus, who is the eternal living water—eternal life itself, her objective had totally changed! With a new glow on her face, she told everyone that the man she had never met before knew everything about her past and that He was the Messiah that they'd all been waiting for.

"Come, see a man who told me all the things that I have done; this is not the Christ, is it?" These words were enough to arouse the townspeople's curiosity.

My Food is to Do the Will of Him

"Meanwhile the disciples were urging Him, saying, 'Rabbi, eat.' But He said to them, 'I have food to eat that you do not know about.' So the disciples were saying to one another, 'No one brought Him anything to eat, did he?' Jesus said to them, 'My food is to do the will of Him who sent Me and to accomplish His work.'" (4:31-34)

While the Samaritan woman ran into town, Jesus' disciples urge Him to eat the food they had brought. But Jesus tells them He has food to eat. "I have food to eat that you do not know about."

At first it seems like Jesus is turning down the food that the disciples sought hard to bring, but this is not the case. Jesus was using this opportune time when they were all hungry to teach them about "spiritual food" in a way that would be engraved in their hearts. But not understanding their teacher's intentions, they all interpret His Words in their own way. Then they ask each other, "No one brought Him anything to eat, did he?"

The disciples, whose spiritual eyes hadn't been opened yet, were talking about food for the body, whereas Jesus was talking about spiritual food that gives eternal life. Jesus says that spiritual food is doing God's will and completing His work. Then what is God's will and God's work?

In 1 Thessalonians 5:16-18 it says, *"Rejoice always; pray without ceasing; in everything give thanks; for this is God's will for you in Christ Jesus."* And in 1 Thessalonians 4:3, it says, *"For this is the will of God, your sanctification ..."* So being joyful, praying, and giving thanks always, and sanctifying our hearts is the will of God. Furthermore, acting according to God's Words, for example, loving one another, being at peace with and forgiving one another, is also the will of God.

And what is God's work? It is worshipping, evangelizing, dedicating and serving in order to fulfill God's kingdom. However, even if we do a lot of God's work, if we do it with evil in our hearts and continue to sin, we are not doing God's will; therefore our work is in vain. God searches for a clean, good heart of truth. When doing God's work, we must do it according to His will. Only then can our hearts be filled with the joy and fullness of the Holy Spirit; and as a result, receive the answers to our hearts' desires.

The Sower and the Reaper

"Do you not say, 'There are yet four months, and then comes the harvest'? Behold, I say to you, lift up

your eyes and look on the fields, that they are white for harvest. Already he who reaps is receiving wages and is gathering fruit for life eternal; so that he who sows and he who reaps may rejoice together." (4:35-36)

After telling His disciples about spiritual food, He goes on to share an illustration about the "harvest", talking about the sower and the reaper. Depending on the seed, some crops are harvested faster, and others much later. And why do you think Jesus said, "There are yet four months, and then comes the harvest"?

In most cases, the words and numbers recorded in the Bible have a deep spiritual significance, so we need to make sure we try to understand this with the fullness of the Holy Spirit. In 2 Peter 3:8, it says, *"with the Lord one day is like a thousand years, and a thousand years like one day"*; and in Daniel 9:27 it also says that one day is calculated as a year, and seven years is calculated as one week. So "Four months" in this case signifies four thousand years.

From the time the first man, Adam, sinned and was banned from the Garden of Eden, through the time Abraham became the father of faith, until the time Jesus came to this earth, was approximately a span of four thousand years. From the time God began the cultivation of man in order to earn true children, until the time that Jesus our Savior came, the passage of four thousand years went by.

After Jesus came, the process of harvesting the cultivated souls began. Because Jesus redeemed mankind from their sins, those who accept Him are forgiven of their sins and are saved through faith. So "There are yet four months, and then comes the harvest" means four thousand years after the cultivation of man, the way of salvation was opened through our Savior Jesus Christ.

So who are the "sowers", and who are the "reapers"? One of the sowers is God, who sent His Son Jesus into this world. The other sower is Jesus, who became one grain of wheat by dying on the cross and opening the way of salvation. And we, the children of God, are the reapers that harvest those souls that have grown into choice grain. In other words, as the reapers, we can lead many souls to the path to salvation.

"Already he who reaps is receiving wages" means that the reaper has already received salvation through faith. Ephesians 2:8 says, *"For by grace you have been saved through faith; and that not of yourselves, it is the gift of God."* And in Romans 3:24, it is written, *"...being justified as a gift by His grace through the redemption which is in Christ Jesus."*

Salvation is a free gift from God. Although we should have faced eternal death because of our sins, through faith in Jesus Christ, we have received the "wages", or the wonderful grace of salvation. That is why we work hard to share the gospel; so other people can also receive eternal life with us. This is "harvesting the crop for eternal life."

When we—out of thanksgiving for the grace of salvation given to us—diligently share the gospel and reap grain, God rejoices in Heaven (Luke 15:7). We, the spreaders of the gospel, also rejoice with Him. In 3 John 1:3, John talked about this joy, *"For I was very glad when brethren came and testified to your truth, that is, how you are walking in truth."*

"For in this case the saying is true, 'One sows and another reaps.' I sent you to reap that for which you have not labored; others have labored and you have entered into their labor." (4:37-38)

Many people reap what Jesus has sown; however this is not the fruit of our labor or sacrifice. This is the result of Jesus dying on the cross. Also, many of Jesus' disciples, and other people were martyred while spreading the gospel. Even in the Old Testament, there were prophets who—out of their love for God—tried to lead their people to the way of truth, but were persecuted. These people are the sowers.

The apostle Paul said, *"I planted, Apollos watered, but God was causing the growth"* (1 Corinthians 3:6). Anyone can water and reap, but the prophets, Jesus, and Jesus' disciples were the ones who sowed. But this doesn't mean that there are no more sowers today. God still sows through certain servants that He acknowledges. However, most people today only water and reap what's already been sown.

Many Samaritans Believe in Jesus

"From that city many of the Samaritans believed in Him because of the word of the woman who testified, 'He told me all the things that I have done.' So when the Samaritans came to Jesus, they were asking Him to stay with them; and He stayed there two days. Many more believed because of His word; and they were saying to the woman, 'It is no longer because of what you said that we believe, for we have heard for ourselves and know that this One is indeed the Savior of the world.'" (4:39-42)

While Jesus was teaching His disciples about the spiritual world, the Samaritan woman went into town, and, in the most excited tone, she told everyone she met that she had met the Messiah. After hearing the woman's testimony, many Samaritans came to believe in Jesus.

Some people assume that since the Samaritan woman had five husbands, her life was not very exemplary. And they also say that the reason she went to the well at midday was to avoid contact with other people. If this presumption was true, she would be ridiculed by the townspeople, and they probably wouldn't have even listened to her. And when she shouted, "Come and see!" they probably wouldn't have cared what she was saying. But the important fact here is that the townspeople trusted what the woman said and believed her.

From this we can see that the woman was normally acknowledged and trusted by the people. That's why her evangelism was more effective, and the people believed what she said. And as a result of this woman's testimony, many people came to accept Jesus as their Savior. And after receiving God's grace, they urged Jesus to stay with them a little longer so they could listen to His words. Seeing the people's good and earnest heart, Jesus stays to share the gospel to them.

Then the people said to the woman, "It is no longer because of what you said that we believe, for we have heard for ourselves and know that this One is indeed the Savior of the world." At first they believed because of what the woman said, but after meeting Jesus and listening to His words, they were able to truly believe from the center of their hearts that He really was the Messiah who came to save them.

The Second Sign in Cana

What an amazing blessing it is that many people in Sychar came to believe in Jesus through one Samaritan woman! Because of the people's earnest desire for the truth, Jesus stayed with them and shared the gospel for two days before leaving for Galilee.

Why a Prophet Has No Honor in His Own Country

"After the two days He went forth from there into Galilee. For Jesus Himself testified that a prophet has no honor in his own country. So when He came to Galilee, the Galileans received Him, having seen all the things that He did in Jerusalem at the feast; for they themselves also went to the feast." (4:43-45)

From Samaria, Jesus went straight to Galilee without stopping by Nazareth, His hometown. This is because the people of His hometown rejected Jesus. Once, when Jesus was teaching the people of Nazareth, they felt convicted in their hearts and they tried to drive Him out of their town. Not only that, they even took Him to the top of a hill to throw Him off the cliff (Luke 4:16-30).

The people rejected Jesus because they couldn't understand how someone who grew up with them and was the son of a mere carpenter could be their Messiah or prophet (Matthew 13:53-58). They didn't see with their spiritual eyes all the signs He was performing; they were simply looking at Him with their physical eyes.

However, Jesus was welcomed everywhere else. Especially the people who lived in the shores of the lake of Galilee welcomed Jesus. After seeing all the signs and wonders Jesus performed in Jerusalem during the Passover, those Galileans knew He was not just a regular person.

The Royal Official Who Came to Visit Jesus

"Therefore He came again to Cana of Galilee where He had made the water wine. And there was a royal official whose son was sick at Capernaum. When he heard that Jesus had come out of Judea into Galilee, he went to Him and was imploring Him to come down and

heal his son; for he was at the point of death." (4:46- 47)

Upon arriving in Galilee, Jesus goes to Cana, a town within Galilee. This is the place where Jesus performed His first sign turning water into wine (John chapter 2). A royal official of King Herod heard that Jesus came to Cana, and he traveled all the way from Capernaum to visit Him. His son was sick and close to death.

Capernaum is approximately 32km away from Cana; not an easy distance to travel back and forth. As the king's royal official, he could have had his son treated by the best doctors of that time. And, at the time, Jesus was accused of being "demon-possessed" by the chief priests, scribes and other leaders.

However, this man had heard about the signs and wonders Jesus was performing, like turning water into wine, and healing the sick. So, he came to Jesus with a pure, believing heart. He sincerely believed that Jesus would heal his son, so he begged Jesus to come and heal his son.

"So Jesus said to him, 'Unless you people see signs and wonders, you simply will not believe.' The royal official said to Him, 'Sir, come down before my child dies.'" (4:48-49)

The royal official is in an emergency situation where his son could die any minute. But instead of following him right away, Jesus says, "Unless you people see signs and wonders, you simply will not believe." To a man full of worry and fear for his son, he probably can't even comprehend these words. "Sir, come down before my child dies."

Oftentimes there are people around us who open their hearts and accept the Lord without seeing any signs or wonders. But without experiencing signs and wonders, it's very easy for them to have faith based on their own knowledge, which is flesh-based faith. On the contrary, people who experience God's signs and wonders understand that when God intervenes, anything can happen, and thus they gain true faith, or spiritual faith. Therefore these people more readily live according to God's Word.

Of course some people doubt even after seeing signs or wonders occur right before their eyes, but people with good hearts grow in faith when they witness God's signs and wonders. This is the reason why Jesus performed signs and wonders wherever He went.

The royal official had a good heart—that's why he believed all the news about Jesus' signs; however, he did not have true faith. We can see this because he asks Jesus to come before his son dies.

If he truly believed in God the Almighty who could even bring the dead back to life, he wouldn't worry even if his son dies. This is the limitation of a faith based on knowledge. Even after hearing about the almighty power of God, when a person with flesh-based faith reaches a certain point, he cannot show any more faith. Only when he breaks through this point can he experience the miracle according to his faith. This is the true faith that allows one to see God's glory. That's why Jesus says, *"'If you can?' All things are possible to him who believes,"* (Mark

9:23) and *"Go; it shall be done for you as you have believed"* (Matthew 8:13).

Jesus Instantly Heals With His Words

"Jesus said to him, 'Go; your son lives.' The man believed the word that Jesus spoke to him and started off. As he was now going down, his slaves met him, saying that his son was living. So he inquired of them the hour when he began to get better. Then they said to him, 'Yesterday at the seventh hour the fever left him.'" (4:50-52)

Jesus doesn't blame the royal official for his knowledge-based faith. Instead, seeing his sincerity in travelling all the way from Capernaum, He answers his request.

"Go; your son lives." He didn't see his son getting better with his own eyes, but believing in Jesus' words, he returns to Capernaum. While he was still on his way home, he saw familiar faces in the distance. His servants, who should have been taking care of his son, were running towards him.

They were rushing to tell him that his son was well. The official believed in Jesus' words, but how overwhelmingly happy he must have been to hear firsthand that his son was well! Calming his heart, he asked about his son's condition, and he also asked at what time his son had become better. He heard that his son, who had been near death due to high fever, had gotten better the moment Jesus said, "Go; your son lives."

"So the father knew that it was at that hour in which Jesus said to him, 'Your son lives'; and he himself believed and his whole household. This is again a second sign that Jesus performed when He had come out of Judea into Galilee." (4:53-54)

If the royal official had doubted, even after hearing Jesus' Words, his son probably would not have been healed. Because he showed his faith through his actions to the end, he experienced his son's miraculous healing, as well as receiving the blessing of his whole family coming to believe in Jesus. After the sign of turning water into wine, healing the royal official's son was the second sign Jesus performed in Cana.

Like so, faith turns the impossible into possible. Jesus said, *"Therefore I say to you, all things for which you pray and ask, believe that you have received them, and they will be granted you"* (Mark 11:24). This Scripture does not say, "Believe that you will receive them," in the future tense. It says, "Believe that you have received them" in the perfect tense. This means that you must pray believing that you have already received the answer.

The Bible says, *"But he must ask in faith without any doubting, for the one who doubts is like the surf of the sea, driven and tossed by the wind. For that man ought not to expect that he will receive anything from the Lord"* (James 1:6-7). When we pray with full faith in God the Almighty without doubting even a little bit, that's when miraculous signs happen.

Chapter 5

The Sign
at the Pool of Bethesda

1. The Man Who Was Healed after 38 Years of Sickness
(5:1-15)

2. The Jews Who Persecuted Jesus
(5:16-30)

3. Jesus' Testimony for the Jews
(5:31-47)

The Man Who Was Healed
after 38 Years of Sickness

After performing His second sign at Galilee, Jesus went up to Jerusalem. There are several festivals that every Jewish adult male must keep sacred: the Passover, the Feast of Weeks, and the Feast of Tabernacles. So following God's will, Jesus went to Jerusalem to participate in the festivals.

The People Who Gathered Around the Pool of Bethesda

"After these things there was a feast of the Jews, and Jesus went up to Jerusalem. Now there is in Jerusalem by the sheep gate a pool, which is called in Hebrew Bethesda, having five porticoes. In these lay a multitude of those who were sick, blind, lame, and withered, [waiting for the moving of the waters; for an angel of the Lord went down at certain seasons into the pool and stirred up the water; whoever then first, after the stirring up of the water, stepped in was made well from whatever disease with which he was afflicted.]" (5:1-4)

The Jerusalem temple has several gates. One of the gates, which is located on the northeast side of the temple, was called the "Sheep Gate". Built during Nehemiah's time, around 445 B.C. (Nehemiah 3:1), it was named the "Sheep Gate" because just outside of the gate was a livestock market, and so sheep needed for sacrificial worship were brought in through this gate. Next to the Sheep Gate is a pool which in Hebrew is called "Bethesda". This pool was created as a type of reservoir which collects rainwater and provides water to the whole temple. The interesting thing about this pool was that occasionally, clear spring water would shoot up from the bottom of the pool and move the water inside the pool. People believed that this was caused by an angel coming down and stirring the water. And the first person to go into the pool right after this happened would be healed of whatever disease he had. This is why the pool was always crowded with the sick. The blind, the lame, the withered—people with all kinds of diseases—waited by the pool, waiting for the waters to stir.

The ancient Biblical manuscripts do not have the words, "waiting for the moving of the waters; for an angel of the Lord went down at certain seasons into the pool and stirred

: : The Sheep Gate located on the northeastern side wall of Jerusalem

: : The Pool of Bethesda located near the Sheep Gate

up the water; whoever then first, after the stirring up of the water, stepped in was made well from whatever disease with which he was afflicted." However, this passage showed up in later manuscripts, which is an implication that this was just a popular belief among the people at the time. As God's Word, the Bible does not have even the slightest error; however, from time to time, there are words recorded in it to help the reader better understand and experience the circumstances of that time period.

Jesus, Who Healed the Sick on the Sabbath Day

"A man was there who had been ill for thirty-eight years. When Jesus saw him lying there, and knew that he had already been a long time in that condition, He said to him, 'Do you wish to get well?' The sick man answered Him, 'Sir, I have no man to put me into the pool when the water is stirred up, but while I am coming, another steps down before me.' Jesus said to him, 'Get up, pick up your pallet and walk.' Immediately the man became well, and picked up his pallet and began to walk. Now it was the Sabbath on that day." (5:5-9)

The porticoes of Bethesda were always crowded with invalids. In order to be the first to enter the pool after the waters are stirred, people tried to get as close to the pool as possible. Among them was one man who had been sick for 38 years.

There is an old Korean saying, "Long illness has no faithful child," meaning even the most faithful person cannot continue to be faithful and dutiful if his parent's illness lasts an unbearably long time. Being sick for 38 years, this man was probably already abandoned by his family and without a single person to help him. However, in the midst of great pain and suffering, he had not given up hope. With the hope of getting well someday, he stayed by the pool. Seeing this man's heart that had waited patiently without losing hope, Jesus reached out to the man with love.

"Do you wish to get well?"

Having been deprived of such gentle words for a long time, he replies, explaining his unfortunate situation. Even when the waters were stirred, someone else, who was more able than he, would go into the pool before him. He was asking Jesus to help him into the pool, but what Jesus said next took the man by surprise.

"Get up, pick up your pallet and walk."

To someone who had been living as a handicap for a long time, this might sound bizarre. He might even think Jesus was mocking him. But, before he knew it, he was on his feet! Somehow, strength was restored in his body. Jesus only spoke a few words, and the illness that had bothered the man for 38 years left him instantly! Jesus didn't cure just anyone. He only healed people after looking at their faith and deeds. Jesus healed this man because, despite his long suffering, his heart was good. It was persevering and hopeful.

The Jews Who Did Not Understand the True Meaning of the Sabbath

> "So the Jews were saying to the man who was cured, 'It is the Sabbath, and it is not permissible for you to carry your pallet.'" But he answered them, 'He who made me well was the one who said to me, "Pick up your pallet and walk."' They asked him, 'Who is the man who said to you, "Pick up your pallet and walk"?' But the man who was healed did not know who it was, for Jesus had slipped away while there was a crowd in that place." (5:10-13)

The man who had been an invalid for 38 years had no reason to stay by the pool anymore. As he picked up his pallet to leave, the Jews approached him. This is because the day the man was healed was the Sabbath day, and the traditions of the elders strictly forbade even moving objects on that day. The Israelites experienced hardship every time they disobeyed God's commandments, or His laws. When a king who feared God was on the throne, Israel had peace. But when a king who didn't fear God and worshiped false idols, was on the throne, Israel was conquered by other nations and its people taken as captives. So in order to obey God's laws more strictly, the Israelites had modified the commandments to include much more specific details. This is referred to in the Bible as the "tradition of the elders".

So for instance, in order to abide by the commandment, "Keep the Sabbath Day holy," the Jews added several subdivisions to this commandment, listing in detail things they should refrain from. They added detailed articles to the commandment such as: one should not sow seeds or plow a field, nor knead dough or bake, one should not do laundry, nor write two words or erase them, one should not brush, or move an object to another place, etc.

However, God never said, "Do not pick up your pallet and walk on the Sabbath Day." God commanded His people to keep the Sabbath Day holy to bless them and to keep that day sacred, but not understanding the true meaning of His commandments, the Jews created these meticulous rules, making it hard on themselves. When they heard that an invalid of 38 years was healed, they should have been happy for him, but instead, the Jews condemned this event.

"It is the Sabbath, and it is not permissible for you to carry your pallet."

The Jews, who had become distressed, persisted with their case.

"Who is the man who said to you, 'Pick up your pallet and walk'?"

Fortunately, Jesus, knowing ahead of time that the Jews would react sensitively to His healing the sick on the Sabbath, had already slipped away when the Jews began their questioning. Jesus did not slip away because He was weak or powerless. Even when He was being unjustly persecuted, He only acted with righteousness. No matter what situation He was in, He never did anything that might hinder the fulfillment of God's will.

"You Have Become Well; Do Not Sin Anymore."

"Afterward Jesus found him in the temple and said to him, 'Behold, you have become well; do not sin anymore, so that nothing worse happens to you.' The man went away, and told the Jews that it was Jesus who had made him well." (5:14-15)

When Jesus met the man who had been an invalid for 38 years at the temple once again, He warned him, "Do not sin anymore, so that nothing worse happens to you."

Jesus was teaching the man that yes, God did heal him. However, if he does not live according to God's Word and sins again, he will be inflicted with a more serious illness. So here, we can see that sickness comes from sin. This is the same not only with sicknesses, but with all other problems as well. When we love and fear God and we live according to His will, diseases and infirmities cannot come near us, and we receive a blessing of prosperity in all areas of our lives.

But if we do not live according to the Word, we come to suffer from all kinds of diseases and problems. Most often, people think that one gets sick because of bad luck or because it's hereditary. However, the cause of even hereditary diseases is many times related to the sin of not abiding by God's Word. If for example, we eat our meals irregularly, or if we are given to gluttony, first our digestive system, and eventually all the organs in our bodies become weak. This is due to our failure to take good care of our bodies which God gave us. So, this is the same thing as being disobedient to God's Word.

In Exodus 15:26, it says, *"If you will give earnest heed to the voice of the LORD your God, and do what is right in His sight, and give ear to His commandments, and keep all His statutes, I will put none of the diseases on you which I have put on the Egyptians; for I, the LORD, am your healer."* When we abide by God's laws and live acceptable lives before God, He will heal any diseases we may have and make us whole.

The man didn't even know who it was that healed him. But after meeting Jesus again at the temple and learning that it was He who healed him, he was overjoyed. When they asked, he gladly told the Jews that it was Jesus who had healed him, but he did not know of their intentions. He didn't know that his words could harm Jesus in any way.

After healing someone, there are times when Jesus tells the person to go tell his relatives, and then there are times when He tells them not to tell anyone about it (Matthew 8:4; Luke 8:56). If the other person hearing about the miracle has a good heart and is someone who would give glory to God and have faith in Him, then Jesus told the healed person to tell him or her. However, if the person hearing about it is someone who would persecute the other person or cause harm to them because of what happened, then Jesus told him not to tell anyone. This is why it's important to be wise when we share information with someone—by first fathoming their heart.

The Jews Who Persecuted Jesus

Jesus was persecuted by the Jews for performing a miracle on the Sabbath Day. Not understanding the laws correctly, they condemned Jesus, who performed a good deed. However, Jesus says in Mark 2:27-28, *"The Sabbath was made for man, and not man for the Sabbath. So the Son of Man is Lord even of the Sabbath."*

Being Lord of the Sabbath, Jesus healed the people suffering from diseases and showed love that surpassed even the laws. Like this, God favors love and compassion over the laws.

"For this reason the Jews were persecuting Jesus, because He was doing these things on the Sabbath. But He answered them, 'My Father is working until now, and I Myself am working.' For this reason therefore the

Jews were seeking all the more to kill Him, because He not only was breaking the Sabbath, but also was calling God His own Father, making Himself equal with God."(5:16-18)

A good person does not judge or condemn others. Instead, he tries hard to understand others by putting himself in their shoes. However, the Jews were trying to pick a quarrel with Jesus and persecute Him for doing a good deed. To this, Jesus says, "My Father is working until now, and I Myself am working," and He stresses the fact that He's not acting according to His own will. When they heard this, the Jews became furious and sought even more to kill Jesus. To them, it appeared that Jesus not only broke the Sabbath, but by calling God His own Father, He was making Himself equal to God.

However, fundamentally, Jesus and God are one. He was with God from the beginning, and He saw how the universe was created and maintained. Because He saw everything from start to finish and knew everything from the beginning, He always acted according to God's will, and never did anything that went against God's will or plan. The Jews, who were spiritually blind, could not understand this fact. On top of that, Jesus was doing things that they themselves could not do, and was receiving praise from the people, so they became envious and jealous.

Jesus Tries to Help the Jews Understand

"Therefore Jesus answered and was saying to them, 'Truly, truly, I say to you, the Son can do nothing of Himself, unless it is something He sees the Father doing; for whatever the Father does, these things the Son also does in like manner. For the Father loves the Son, and shows Him all things that He Himself is doing; and the Father will show Him greater works than these, so that you will marvel.'" (5:19-20)

Let's say a father who owns a huge company wants to pass the business to his son. He will teach his son everything he needs to know about running the business and even the company's top secret information too. Likewise, God taught his loving Son, Jesus, who was with Him from the beginning (from creation to cultivation of man), His providence, and all the secrets of creation. Jesus came to this world to show us what the Father God had taught and showed Him. By healing the sick, raising the dead back to life, and by calming the winds and the waters, He performed amazing wonders (Luke 8:24).

And to the people who were all astonished with what He did, He prophesized that they would see even greater things through which they would marvel. By this He was referring to the event where He would be taking up the sins of all the people by dying on the cross and resurrecting again on the third day. On top of that, Jesus being lifted up to Heaven after resurrecting would have been an event of such marvel, and an event that no one has seen before. Jesus coming back to this world in the end time will also be an inspiring and marvelous event.

The Relationship between the Father and the Son

"'For just as the Father raises the dead and gives them life, even so the Son also gives life to whom He wishes. For not even the Father judges anyone, but He has given all judgment to the Son, so that all will honor the Son even as they honor the Father. He who does not honor the Son does not honor the Father who sent Him.'" (5:21-23)

God, who has supreme authority over a person's life and death, also gave that authority to His Son, Jesus. So when Jesus says, "The Son also gives life to whom He wishes," He means that Jesus can give life to whomever He wants.

So what does it mean when the Scripture says that God has given all judgment to the Son? As Romans 3:10 says, *"There is none righteous; not even one,"* after the fall of Adam, all mankind had to go the way of death. But the God of love prepared a way of salvation for us; and that way is Jesus Christ. So whoever believes in Him and lives according to His Word go to Heaven, and those who do not go to Hell. This is why the Scripture says, "He [God] has given all judgment to the Son." This means that God's will is Jesus' will.

As it is written in Romans 5:1, *"Therefore, having been*

justified by faith, we have peace with God through our Lord Jesus Christ," Jesus is the bridge of faith that connects our relationship with God. When we believe and obey Jesus' words, then we are believing and obeying God's Word. That is why knowing and honoring Jesus Christ is, in essence, knowing and honoring God.

When Hearing the Voice of God's Son

"'Truly, truly, I say to you, he who hears My word, and believes Him who sent Me, has eternal life, and does not come into judgment, but has passed out of death into life. Truly, truly, I say to you, an hour is coming and now is, when the dead will hear the voice of the Son of God, and those who hear will live. For just as the Father has life in Himself, even so He gave to the Son also to have life in Himself; and He gave Him authority to execute judgment, because He is the Son of Man." (5:24-27)

Whoever listens to the words of Jesus and believes in God who sent Him will not come into judgment; but pass from death to life. The word "believes" in this Scripture doesn't just mean faith that is justified by saying with one's lips, "I believe." It signifies the belief that comes from "spiritual faith" that is justified by one's actions that are in accordance with God's Word.

"The dead" does not refer to physically dead people, but people who are spiritually dead. When God created people, He created them to be a living being with a spirit, soul, and body. But when the first man, Adam, disobeyed God, sin entered man, and his spirit died.

So all of Adam's descendants are born with original sin and their spirits are dead; however, when they hear the gospel and accept Jesus Christ as their Savior and receive the Holy Spirit, their spirits are revived. And when they act according to God's Word and transform more and more into a person of truth, or a person of spirit, this is what the Scripture refers to as hearing the voice of God's Son. And the Lord says an hour is coming and now is when people hear the voice of God's Son.

He also says, "For just as the Father has life in Himself, even so He gave to the Son also to have life in Himself." The life here refers to eternal, spiritual life, which does not perish. And Jesus, who is one with God, also has life in Him (John 14:6), so if we believe in Him and accept Him, we also gain eternal life.

And because Jesus is the Son of Man, God gave Him the authority to execute judgment; and this judgment is made according to a person's life. Meaning, a person who believes in Jesus Christ has life, and therefore goes to Heaven; and a person who does not believe in Jesus Christ and doesn't have this life goes to Hell. So why did God give His Son this authority to execute judgment?

Just as we need to put an object on a scale to measure its weight, we also need a standard by which we can judge whether a person has life or not. Jesus Christ is the scale of life, and the standard for judgment. This is because Jesus alone is life, or truth itself. And that is why God gave His Son the authority to execute judgment.

The Resurrection of Life and the Resurrection of Judgment

> "Do not marvel at this; for an hour is coming, in which all who are in the tombs will hear His voice, and will come forth; those who did the good deeds to a resurrection of life, those who committed the evil deeds to a resurrection of judgment. I can do nothing on My own initiative. As I hear, I judge; and My judgment is just, because I do not seek My own will, but the will of Him who sent Me." (John 5:28-30)

When they are told that life and judgment depends on God's Son, some people are in disbelief. They ask, "Then what happens to all the people that lived and died before Jesus was born?" That is why Jesus says, "Do not marvel at this," and then He tells us about the judgment of conscience.

It has only been a hundred some years since Christianity came into Korea. Then what would happen to those people who lived one hundred years ago, or the people of the Old Testament times? If all these people are sent to Hell just because they did not know Jesus Christ, then how can we say God is love?

God, who is love itself, prepared a way of salvation for those people with good hearts. For those people who did good deeds during their lifetime, they will experience a resurrection of life, and those who did evil deeds would experience a resurrection of judgment (Romans 2:14-16). So the "judgment of conscience" is a way of salvation that God prepared for those who lived during the Old Testament times before Jesus came, and those who lived during the New Testament times and never had the chance to hear the gospel.

Even though they never heard the gospel, there are people who stand in awe and have a reverent fear of heaven, and make every effort to try to live a good and righteous life, and therefore live according to God's will to a certain extent (Ecclesiastes 3:11; Romans 1:20). There are some people who sacrifice their lives for their country, or their parents, or even their friends. This is sacrificial love.

If these kinds of people hear the gospel, wouldn't they, for sure, accept the Lord, receive salvation, and enter Heaven? So through the judgment of conscience, God allows these people to receive salvation (Refer to the book, *Hell*).

This is how the God of justice gives everyone a fair judgment. When Jesus talked about the judgment, the people listening were suddenly gripped with fear, and they wondered, "What will this judgment be like?" Knowing the question on their minds, Jesus answered, "I can do nothing on My own initiative. As I hear, I judge; and My judgment is just, because I do not seek My own will, but the will of Him who sent Me."

Jesus' Testimony for the Jews

The prophets of the Old Testament and John the Baptist had already spread the word about Jesus. They prophesied that Jesus would be born from the family of Jesse, and that the nations would resort to Him, that He would be born in Bethlehem, and that 'His goings forth are from long ago, from the days of eternity' (Isaiah 11:10; Micah 5:2). These prophets did not speak on their own accord. God had them tell these prophecies for Jesus Christ.

In addition to these prophecies, the signs and wonders that Jesus performed speak for themselves: that Jesus came from God. But the Jews still didn't recognize Him and began to persecute Him, so He showed evidence that He is God's Son. He did this only out of love for them, so that they might receive salvation.

"There Is Another Who Testifies of Me"

"If I alone testify about Myself, My testimony is not true. There is another who testifies of Me, and I know that the testimony which He gives about Me is true. You have sent to John, and he has testified to the truth. But the testimony which I receive is not from man, but I say these things so that you may be saved." (5:31-34)

Imagine how embarrassing and funny it would look if someone was boasting about himself, but no one took notice? So even if we had enough confidence to boast about ourselves, we have to first be recognized by the people around us. Jesus had every right to boast about Himself, but He only waited for God to show others who He was. Instead of testifying about Himself, Jesus used the signs which God manifested through Him to speak for them.

Then why do you think Jesus said He does not receive testimony from man? This is because there wasn't anyone who could give a complete and accurate testimony about Jesus at that time. Even John the Baptist couldn't give a perfect testimony about Jesus. That is why while John was in prison he sent his disciples to ask Jesus, *"Are You the Expected One, or shall we look for someone else?"* (Matthew 11:3).

To this, Jesus replied in the following verses 4-5, *"GGo and report to John what you hear and see: the blind receive sight and the lame walk, the lepers are cleansed and the deaf hear, the dead are raised up, and the poor have the gospel preached to them."* He said this because just knowing this fact would let them know, "Oh, this is definitely the One that God sent."

Spiritual things can only be discerned by spiritual minds (1 Corinthians 2:13); but at the time, people didn't know that Jesus was of God. Therefore it was even hard for them to accurately testify about Jesus. In order to lead as many people to salvation as possible, Jesus talked a lot about the evidence and works of God. But, the Jews who were full of jealousy misunderstood this to be Jesus boasting about Himself and knowing this very well, Jesus said that the testimony He receives is not from man.

Wonders and Signs: God's Works

"He was the lamp that was burning and was shining and you were willing to rejoice for a while in his light. But the testimony which I have is greater than the testimony of John; for the works which the Father has given Me to accomplish—the very works that I do— testify about Me, that the Father has sent Me." (5:35-36)

A lamp goes out when it runs out of oil. Jesus compares John to a lamp because his life was short. John was born 6 months before Jesus, but during Jesus' public ministry—when John was only in his early thirties—his life was ended by Herod Antipas.

But during his short lifetime, John rebuked sinners and lawbreakers testifying the truth, just like a lamp that gives light in the darkness (John 5:33). As a lamp preparing for the way of the Lord, he pointed out people's sins and led them to repent and come out into righteousness.

As mentioned earlier, after the prophet Malachi, Israel was in spiritual darkness for 400 years, and John was actually the first prophet to proclaim God's Word again. So his popularity was high. Because John became like a lamp, the people enjoyed seeing this light, but John's cry for righteousness was transient; for he was proclaiming about someone who would be coming after him, who was Jesus.

So evidence that would be more accurate than John's testimony would be the actual works of God that Jesus Himself performs. Through numerous signs and wonders, Jesus shows the people evidence that God is with Him.

The Scriptures Testify About Jesus

"And the Father who sent Me, He has testified of Me. You have neither heard His voice at any time nor seen His form. You do not have His word abiding in you, for you do not believe Him whom He sent. You search the Scriptures because you think that in them you have eternal life; it is these that testify about Me; and you are unwilling to come to Me so that you may have life. I do not receive glory from men; but I know you, that you do not have the love of God in yourselves. I have come in My Father's name, and you do not receive Me; if another comes in his own name, you will receive him." (5:37-43)

God testified about Jesus through many signs and wonders, but the Pharisees, Sadducees, and the teachers of the law did not believe in Him. To this Jesus says they have 'neither heard His voice at any time nor seen His form'. He adds that this is because they do not have His Word abiding in them. These people pride themselves in knowing more of God's Word than anyone else. Why would Jesus tell these people, "You do not have His word abiding in you"?

When receiving God's Word, depending on whether a person receives it with a good heart or an evil heart, the outcome is totally different. These people knew very well that God would be sending them the Messiah, as prophesied in the Old Testament. However, instead of receiving these words with an understanding of God's heart, they received them according to their own thoughts and ways that benefit themselves; so when the actual Messiah stood in front of them, they could not recognize Him, and did not accept Him. Because of their pride in knowing the Law, and because of their selfishness in trying to keep their place in society, they actually persecuted Jesus. That's why Jesus said God's Word is not in them.

Many people think that if they read God's Word in the Bible and listen to sermons they can receive salvation; however this is not true. Only when we understand God's Word and act according to it, can our salvation be made complete (Matthew 7:21). Even if we know for sure where our destination is, if we do not move toward it, we can never reach it. Likewise, if we know we want to go to Heaven, simply knowing God's will won't get us there. We need to understand His will and act according to it.

Since these teachers of the law were blinded by their own evil and couldn't recognize Jesus, Jesus spoke to them very firmly, "I do not receive glory from men; but I know you, that you do not have the love of God in yourselves." Jesus does not try to receive glory from people of this world. Glory of this world is vain; and ultimately it's bound to perish.

God does not give us salvation to receive glory. He's offering us salvation simply because He loves us. God wants to share His true love with us who, after receiving salvation, have become His true children. When a person receives salvation and is transformed by the truth, he or she comes to give glory to God, which God receives with much joy.

People who do not accept Jesus do not have love for God. Since they are living in the midst of their own selfishness and are blinded by it, even though Jesus came in the name of God, they don't recognize Him.

If You Believed Moses, You Would Believe Me

"How can you believe, when you receive glory from one another and you do not seek the glory that is from the one and only God? Do not think that I will accuse you before the Father; the one who accuses you is Moses, in whom you have set your hope. For if you believed Moses, you would believe Me, for he wrote about Me. But if you do not believe his writings, how will you believe My words?"(5:44-47)

Depending on the amount of evil we have in our hearts, that's how much we try to fulfill our selfish desires, and for this reason, we cannot love God. At the time, the Jews wanted to gain fame, power, and the like; and they did not seek for the glory that comes from God. So Jesus pointed out what was in their hearts that was causing them to persecute Him and desire His downfall.

So what does it mean when Jesus says, "Your accuser is Moses"? During those times, people diligently read and believed in the laws, because people received salvation based on their deeds, with the Law of Moses being the standard. In court, the defending lawyer defends the accused, while the prosecutor pursues the accused for their wrongdoing. When we stand before God, the Law of Moses acts like a prosecutor that takes legal action against us.

In the future, after the Lord's return, when the Millennium Kingdom comes to an end, there is the Great White Throne Judgment. During this judgment, God will be the judge, and Jesus will be the lawyer. Around God and Jesus, twenty four elders will attend the judgment as the jury, and each person will be judged on how much he or she lived in the truth, based on the Law of Moses. One does not receive salvation simply because he believes in Jesus Christ. His life will be judged in light of the Law.

The Law of Moses was recorded for Jesus Christ. Therefore, Jesus asks the teachers of the law how they can believe His words if they don't believe Moses' writings. If a person believes in the true meaning of the Law, which God gave us, then he will also believe in Jesus Christ, who fulfills the Law. And, if one truly believes from the center of his heart, then like Jesus Christ, he will act in the light, and in righteousness, and go toward the way of salvation.

Chapter 6

The Bread of Life

The Sign of the Two Fish and Five Loaves

The Sea of Galilee is technically a lake, but the Bible refers to it as the "sea", because the lake is very big, and it appears to be a large body of water like the sea, or the ocean. In the Old Testament, it is called Lake Chinneroth, because it is shaped like a harp; and in the New Testament, it is called Lake Gennesaret, and sometimes the Sea of Tiberias. During His public ministry, Jesus travelled around the neighborhoods near the shores of the Sea of Galilee to tell the people about the kingdom of God, and He also performed many signs and wonders wherever He went.

"After these things Jesus went away to the other side of the Sea of Galilee (or Tiberias). A large crowd followed Him, because they saw the signs which He was performing on those who were sick. Then Jesus

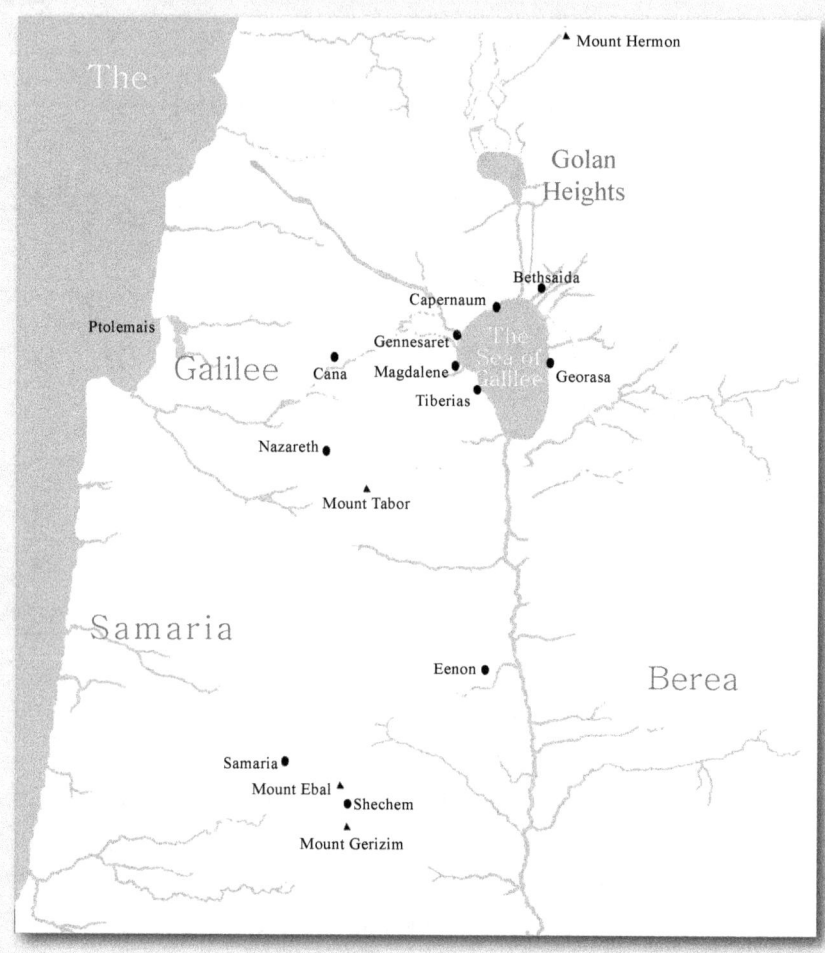

:: The areas around the Sea of Galilee

went up on the mountain, and there He sat down with His disciples. Now the Passover, the feast of the Jews, was near." (6:1-4)

Jesus' twelve disciples also went out in pairs and spread the gospel while showing God's power through signs and wonders. Naturally, the word about Jesus spread rapidly. In order to take a short rest, Jesus and His disciples boarded a boat and left for the city of Bethsaida, a city located on the other side of the Sea of Tiberias. And seeing them leave on the boat, many people from different cities walked out to see them. People actually went ahead of them and waited for them. Seeing the crowd of people awing and admiring after seeing a sign, Jesus felt compassion for them, for they were like sheep without a shepherd. So He healed the sick and enlightened them with many teachings. (Ref: Matthew 14:13-14; Mark 6:30-34; Luke 9:10-11)

It was a couple days before the Passover. The people were listening to the Word of God without realizing the passing of time. As it was getting late, the disciples who were with Jesus began to worry because they were in a large, empty field where there was no food.

Jesus Tests Phillip

"Therefore Jesus, lifting up His eyes and seeing that a large crowd was coming to Him, said to Philip, 'Where are we to buy bread, so that these may eat?' This He was saying to test him, for He Himself knew what He was

**intending to do. Philip answered Him, 'Two hundred
denarii worth of bread is not sufficient for them, for
everyone to receive a little.'" (6:5-7)**

It was late, and the people hadn't eaten the whole day.
Knowing they would be hungry, Jesus asks Phillip, "Where are
we to buy bread, so that these may eat?"

Jesus knew what He was going to do, but He waited for
Phillip's response. He was testing him. Of course Jesus wasn't
trying to put him on the spot; He was simply giving Phillip an
opportunity to observe for himself and acquire greater faith.

Trials can be categorized largely into two types. The first
type is the temptation that comes from the enemy devil when
we don't live according to God's Word (James 1:13-15). The
second type is the test that God gives us in order to bless us; as
in the case of Abraham, when God asked him to sacrifice Isaac,
his only son. If we, with faith, have victory over a trial and are
approved by God, we can receive both spiritual and physical
blessings, just like Abraham, who became the root of blessings.
On the contrary, when we are in trial because of our own faults,
if we repent and obey God's Word, the trial comes to an end,
but we don't receive any special blessings for it.

During all my years in ministry, I experienced many trials
and tribulations. One of these trials was when my three
daughters were victims of carbon monoxide gas poisoning from
briquette gas; and another one was the time I lost so much
blood that I was on the verge of death. Aside from these events,

trials I experienced were so difficult that from the viewpoint of a man of flesh, the sorrow and hardship the trials brought were unbearable. Then there were times when a test was so great that it would have been easier to lay down my life than to get through the test.

However, I was able to get through each test with faith. God did not allow these trials into my life because of some wrongdoing. It was through this process of trials that God increasingly added more and more of His power to my life.

After Jesus' sudden question, Phillip began to calculate. Estimating how much food would be necessary for each person, and counting how many people there were, Phillip answers with confidence:

"Two hundred denarii worth of bread is not sufficient for them, for everyone to receive a little."

The denarius was a monetary currency of the Roman Empire. One denarius was worth one man's daily wage, so two hundred denarii would equal to two hundred days worth of wages. Let's say a daily wage is worth about fifty dollars. Then the amount of money they would have needed would be ten thousand dollars. Phillip's calculation seems pretty reasonable. However, if he had possessed true faith, he wouldn't have used his human reasoning. He would have answered, "I believe You will be able to take care of this."

Phillip hadn't yet realized the limitless power of Jesus, with which nothing is impossible. Many times people try to solve their problems using human knowledge and wisdom; however, man's insight has limitations, so at one point or another, people reach their limit. But if we have spiritual faith, then nothing is impossible (Mark 9:23). Why? Because with God, anything is possible.

The Disciples Who Lacked Spiritual Faith

"One of His disciples, Andrew, Simon Peter's brother, said to Him, 'There is a lad here who has five barley loaves and two fish, but what are these for so many people?' Jesus said, 'Have the people sit down.' Now there was much grass in the place so the men sat down, in number about five thousand." (6:8-10)

While Jesus and Phillip were talking, Andrew walked through the crowd to see if anyone had some food. He checked with many people, but the only food he found was a young boy's lunch consisting of two fish and five barley loaves of bread. Even while telling Jesus what he found, he knew that the food was too little to make any difference. Anyone would have seen that the amount of food that they had was terribly insufficient.

The disciples saw numerous signs and wonders while following Jesus around during His ministry, but still they didn't have complete faith in Him. Many people profess to believe in the almighty God, but when they come face to face with some hardship, they fail to show their faith, and they struggle. His disciples, including Andrew, were displaying faith based on knowledge. They did not have spiritual faith—faith in which one truly believes from the center of his heart and acts upon it.

Jesus had the people sit in groups of hundreds and fifties (Mark 6:40). Since the field was full of grass, it was easy for people to sit in groups. There were so many people that they appeared as waves of water in the vast open field. There were five thousand men, excluding women and children (Matthew 14:21). So there was probably a total of ten thousand people or more. All these people needed to be fed, and yet there were only five barley loaves of bread and two fish.

But to the almighty God, the number of people is not a problem. Whether it's for 10,000 people or 100,000 people, It's not a problem because He can create something from nothing anyway. It's much the same in the case of diseases. The seriousness of the disease does not determine how easy or how difficult it is to receive healing for that disease. It really depends on the individual's faith. To God, all diseases are the same.

Jesus Performs the Sign of the Two Fish and Five Loaves

"Jesus then took the loaves, and having given thanks, He distributed to those who were seated; likewise also of the fish as much as they wanted. When they were filled, He said to His disciples, 'Gather up the leftover fragments so that nothing will be lost.' So they gathered them up, and filled twelve baskets with fragments from the five barley loaves which were left over by those who had eaten." (6:11-13)

Taking the fish and loaves from the disciples, Jesus gave thanks and began to distribute the food to the people. Having followed Jesus around all day, everyone must have been quite hungry! The total amount of food needed to satisfy their hunger would have been unbelievably great. But what happened? Everyone received as much bread and fish as they wanted, and the food did not run out. Over 10,000 people had eaten until they were full, and yet here and there were leftover pieces of food. Jesus told His disciples to gather all the leftovers. Much to their surprise, there were twelve baskets filled with leftover food.

Now there's a reason why Jesus told the disciples to gather the leftovers. The leftover food was evidence of the sign that God showed them. People have a tendency to forget about what happened in the past. Even after witnessing God's power at work, over time, people easily forget about it. If this day had ended with everyone simply eating to their satisfaction, then this event would have been only a wonderful memory for a little while, and then sooner or later it would have been forgotten. But all of the leftover fish and bread was concrete evidence of the fact that God had provided a sign.

And what significance do the twelve baskets have? In the Bible, every number has significance. The number "12" is a number of the light, and it signifies perfection (John 11:9). If you look at the twelve tribes of Israel, the twelve disciples of Jesus, and the twelve pearl gates of New Jerusalem, God uses the number "12" as a sign of promised blessings. So when the Scripture says there were twelve baskets of food leftover, it means that to those people who act completely in the light,

: : The Church of the Multiplication of the Loaves and the Fishes in Tabgha

which is the truth, God will answer them with blessings that overflow.

The People Who Wanted to Make Jesus King

"Therefore when the people saw the sign which He had performed, they said, 'This is truly the Prophet who is to come into the world.' So Jesus, perceiving that they were intending to come and take Him by force to

make Him king, withdrew again to the mountain by Himself alone. (6:14-15)

A sign is something that occurs by God's power which goes far beyond human capabilities. The people who saw the unbelievable sign that had just occurred before their very eyes, began to speak excitedly among themselves. People went into frenzy, shouting, "Not only are incurable diseases being healed, but we can also eat as much as we want, and whenever we want!" They confessed, "This is truly the Prophet who is to come into the world," and the talk about the amazing thing that had just happened began to blossom everywhere.

People had been waiting for a long time for the Messiah that the Prophets of the Old Testament had prophesied about (Deuteronomy 18:15). On top of that, the Israelites were being oppressed by the Romans. Just seeing Jesus, the people realized that He had wisdom, delivered powerful messages, and performed signs. In all areas, no other person could begin to compare with Him. They thought if Jesus became king, He could surely free them from Rome. After witnessing the sign, instead of gaining true faith, the people began to seek for their own glory.

Jesus knew these people wanted to make Him king by force. That is why he told His disciples to take the boat and go to the other side, and after sending the crowds away, He went up to the mountain to pray (Matthew 14:22-23). Jesus did not perform the sign of the two fish and five loaves in order to become king. He only performed the sign to give the people evidence that confirmed the word He was teaching; to make them believe in Himself, the Son of God, and in God who sent Him (John 4:48; Mark 16:20).

Jesus Who Walked on Water, and the Crowd Who Followed Him

The Sea of Galilee is surrounded by tall, steep mountains such as the Golan Heights, and Mount Hermon. It is also about 200 meters below sea level of the Mediterranean. Due to these geographic characteristics, the weather there is very unpredictable. Strong blasts of wind come up and blow here and there frequently and unpredictably.

"Now when evening came, His disciples went down to the sea, and after getting into a boat, they started to cross the sea to Capernaum. It had already become dark, and Jesus had not yet come to them. The sea began to be stirred up because a strong wind was blowing. Then, when they had rowed about three or four miles, they saw Jesus walking on the sea and drawing near to the boat; and they were frightened. But He said to them, 'It is I; do not be afraid.' So they were willing to receive Him into the boat, and immediately the boat was at the land to which they were going." (6:16-21)

As evening drew near, the disciples got on a boat to travel to Capernaum. As usual, the winds were very strong. As time went on, the winds grew stronger and the sea became rough, and the boat carrying the disciples shook above the waves like a fallen leaf on a windy day in autumn. It was pitch black, so the disciples couldn't see anything. When Jesus was with them, they were welcomed everywhere they went, and all was always well. But now, they were alone without Jesus, and fierce winds and waves were hitting them left and right. Naturally, fear took hold of them.

When the disciples were finally able to put the oars in the water and row for about 4 meters, they saw a figure that looked like a person above the dark waters. Seeing the disciples struggling in the turbulence, Jesus had walked on the water to get to them (Matthew 14:25). For a moment, the disciples thought He was a ghost, and they screamed in fear. A man walking on water was an unbelievable sight! So in order to calm the terrified disciples who had not been able to recognize their teacher, Jesus said, "It is I; do not be afraid."

If you look at Matthew 14:28, Peter says to Jesus, *"Lord, if it is You, command me to come to You on the water."* To this, Jesus responded, "Come!" Peter got out of the boat and walked on the water. But soon he saw the raging waters, became frightened and he started to sink into the water. Peter cried out, "Lord save me!" Immediately, Jesus pulled him out of the water and got into the boat with him. The reason why the disciples weren't able to recognize Jesus and became filled with fear is because they incorporated their fleshly thoughts into the situation they were in. A person living in the truth gains boldness before God, so fear cannot enter into them (1 John 3:21-22, 4:18). This is because God always protects and abides with a person who obeys His commands.

Because they saw Jesus in the midst of hardship, the disciples were more overjoyed than ever before. How magnificent would it be, if an unsolvable problem were suddenly resolved by God's power? When Jesus got in the boat, the wind stopped. Then those in the boat bowed to Him and confessed, *"You are certainly God's Son!"*(Matthew 14:33). And before they knew it, their boat had reached the shores of Capernaum.

The People Who Came To Capernaum to Meet Jesus

"The next day the crowd that stood on the other side of the sea saw that there was no other small boat there, except one, and that Jesus had not entered with His disciples into the boat, but that His disciples had gone away alone. There came other small boats from Tiberias near to the place where they ate the bread after the Lord had given thanks. So when the crowd saw that Jesus was not there, nor His disciples, they themselves got into the small boats, and came to Capernaum seeking Jesus. When they found Him on the other side of the sea, they said to Him, 'Rabbi, when did You get here?'" (6:22-25)

The people who experienced the miracle of the two fish and five loaves couldn't forget the strong impression they received there the day before, and they came back to the same location the next day. They were sure that the night before, only the disciples had left for Capernaum in one of the two boats that were at the shore. So they thought, "Since Jesus didn't go with them, maybe we can still meet Him here." However, there was no longer anyone there.

Because one of the two boats was still there, the people were very curious about the whereabouts of Jesus. The one boat that was left there is certain evidence that proves Jesus walked on the water to get to the other side. However, the people who didn't know what occurred the night before were perplexed, and wondered, "What happened?"

Fortunately, at about that same time, other boats came from Tiberias. So the people got into these boats and headed for Capernaum in hopes of finding Jesus. When they arrived, Jesus was there. One boat was still ashore on the other side, and they were very curious as to how Jesus came across the sea without a boat. When they found Him they asked, "Rabbi, when did You get here?"

Jesus knew why they were searching for Him so eagerly. Some followed Him because they were intrigued by His extraordinary teachings and some because they were amazed by the signs He performed. However, the most prominent reasons they sought after Him was for fleshly reasons. They sought Jesus either to be healed of diseases, or to fill their bellies with food. The people didn't follow Jesus because they could gain spiritual understanding, but instead, they followed Him more for personal and physical benefit. If they were seeking Him for spiritual reasons, Jesus would have been more joyful, but the truth of the matter was that their hearts were set on things of the flesh.

What Do We Have to Do to Work the Works of God?

"Jesus answered them and said, 'Truly, truly, I say to you, you seek Me, not because you saw signs, but because you ate of the loaves and were filled. Do not work for the food which perishes, but for the food which endures to eternal life, which the Son of Man will give to you, for on Him the Father, God, has set His seal.' Therefore they said to Him, 'What shall we do, so that we may work the works of God?' Jesus answered and said to them, 'This is the work of God, that you believe in Him whom He has sent.'" (6:26-29)

Jesus said to the people who crossed the sea to Capernaum, "You seek Me, not because you saw signs, but because you ate of the loaves and were filled. Do not work for the food which perishes, but for the food which endures to eternal life, which the Son of Man will give to you, for on Him the Father, God, has set His seal."

Here, "food which perishes" refers to food for the flesh which we intake and digest. At times, people are so focused on food for the flesh, and the things that fulfill the short physical life here on earth, that they end up going towards eternal death. What an unwise thing to do! Of course this does not mean we should not work to earn food for the flesh—it simply means we should put a higher priority on acquiring spiritual food. Jesus promised to give them this spiritual food.

Spiritual food is God's Word, which is the truth. Just as people ingest food to maintain physical life, we must take in God's Word, or the truth, to maintain spiritual life. It is Jesus who is the one who gives this spiritual food. He is the one on whom the Father God "has set His seal." To set a seal means to trust and guarantee the quality of someone or something; so a seal symbolizes "trustworthiness." Thus, this Scripture means that God entrusted Jesus with the mission of the salvation of mankind. Jesus came into this world and bore the afflictions and suffered on the cross for our sins.

Since Jesus told the people not to work for food that perishes, they became troubled. The only reason why they asked, "What shall we do, so that we may work the works of God?" was not because they had faith in Jesus, but because they were astonished by the sign He performed. Knowing their hearts, Jesus answered, "This is the work of God, that you believe in Him whom He has sent."

Today many Christians profess to believe in God. However, there is a difference between truly believing, and just attending church. A person who truly knows and believes in the Lord acts in obedience to God's Word with joy and thanksgiving. They also experience God in their daily lives. However, those who just go back and forth to church without this joy, obedience and thanksgiving, are no different from nonbelievers. If they confess to be Christians, and still fall into despair, complain, and become resentful when faced with a trial or hardship, then they are simply calling on the name of the Lord with their lips, and not truly living in the truth.

Faith is not just habitually attending church for worship. Faith is loving God and acting according to His Word. This is 'working the works of God'. To those asking how to work the works of God, Jesus enlightens them by giving them a spiritual answer. He tells them to believe in Jesus the Christ, the One whom God has sent, and become a holy child of God.

> "So they said to Him, 'What then do You do for a sign, so that we may see, and believe You? What work do You perform? Our fathers ate the manna in the wilderness; as it is written, "He gave them bread out of heaven to eat."' Jesus then said to them, 'Truly, truly, I say to you, it is not Moses who has given you the bread out of heaven, but it is My Father who gives you the true bread out of heaven. For the bread of God is that which comes down out of heaven and gives life to the world.'" (6:30-33)

Even though Jesus gave them a spiritual message, the people still wanted to see a sign with their own eyes. They wondered if maybe Jesus was able to make bread come down from heaven, or perhaps He could perform something even more amazing than that. They did not believe Jesus to be the Son of God, but instead they just believed that He was someone who had extraordinary power that the average person didn't have. They thought of Him as another prophet like Moses, who made manna fall from heaven during the Israelites' Exodus.

Jesus says in Matthew 12:39, *"A wicked and adulterous generation asks for a miraculous sign!"* Someone who is only interested in looking after oneself does not believe even when told spiritual messages, and continues to ask for signs. On the other hand, a person with a good heart is moved simply by the Word of truth itself, and receives Jesus Christ when someone shares the gospel with him. This is the difference between a person of the flesh and a person of spirit.

Knowing what was on the people's minds, Jesus teaches them that Moses did not make the manna come down with his own power; but that it was given by God. In order to show them that there is a spiritual world—even though we cannot see it with our eyes—He emphasizes the fact that the manna came down from heaven, and that they need to believe this with their hearts. And since they could not grasp the things that are spiritual in nature, He compares it to bread. He says that bread that comes from heaven is life, and that bread comes to give eternal life.

I Am the Bread of Life

"Then they said to Him, 'Lord, always give us this bread.' Jesus said to them, 'I am the bread of life; he who comes to Me will not hunger, and he who believes

in Me will never thirst. But I said to you that you have seen Me, and yet do not believe. All that the Father gives Me will come to Me, and the one who comes to Me I will certainly not cast out.'" (6:34-37)

Even though Jesus used bread to illustrate eternal life, the people's minds were still on the bread that they ate heartily the day before. Not understanding the spiritual meaning behind Jesus' Words, they insisted that Jesus give them the bread that they could eat just as Moses had given manna to their ancestors. At this time, Jesus makes an unexpected reply. "I am the bread of life; he who comes to Me will not hunger, and he who believes in Me will never thirst."

Jesus was saying He was the bread of life. When the Scripture says to come to Jesus who is the bread of life, it means to come into the truth (John 14:6). Only when we seek to live in the truth, can we go before the Lord, and have all things in Him. To those who come before the Lord and put everything in His hands while praying and living in the truth, God will protect and bless their families, their workplaces, and all things, both spiritually and physically. Also, as they receive power from above, they can do things that go beyond their limitations, and most importantly, because they have eternal life, their spirit will never go hungry or thirsty again.

But even if we acquire fame, power, and riches in this world, when our life comes to an end, all these things fade away like vapor (James 4:14). As it is written in Ecclesiastes 1:8, *"All things are wearisome; man is not able to tell it. The eye is not satisfied with seeing, nor is the ear filled with hearing,"* even though man acquires many good things, he'll always want more. So a person who works to achieve things of the flesh and does not depend on God will only gain as much as he's worked for, never knowing what lies ahead in the course of life. And at times he may even experience unexpected dangers and pitfalls. On top of that, true satisfaction will be nowhere to be found.

Even though Jesus taught the people about the way that they would never thirst and never go hungry again, the people still sought after what they could eat and have right then and there. People like this, who chase after things of the flesh, have evil in their hearts. For this same reason, even when Jesus showed them amazing signs and wonders, they doubted and did not believe in Him. They listened with one ear, and let it out the other ear. On the contrary, people with good hearts saw the signs and wonders that Jesus performed and they confessed, *"If this man were not from God, He could do nothing,"* and they acknowledged Him as the Son of God (John 9:33). This is why Jesus said, "All that the Father gives Me will come to Me, and the one who comes to Me I will certainly not cast out." People with goodness in their hearts are ready to receive salvation from the center of their hearts. So, when they hear about God's works, they come before Jesus and want to know more. Although someone may not know God now, if he has a heart of goodness he will someday come before Jesus and accept Him as his Savior.

The Lord would never cast out someone who has goodness in his heart. And even if he sinned and grew apart from God, as long as he repents and turns around, God will forgive him and not even remember his sin (Hebrews 8:12). This is the love of God.

Before I met the living God, I also thought, "There is no God. When I die, that's it." However, deep inside my heart, I did not completely deny life after death, and I used to be afraid thinking, "What if there is a hell? What will happen if I die and go to hell?" That is why I tried to live with goodness. And, when God cured all my diseases, I accepted the Lord right away.

I Do the Will of Him Who Sent Me

"For I have come down from heaven, not to do My own will, but the will of Him who sent Me. This is the will of Him who sent Me, that of all that He has given Me I lose nothing, but raise it up on the last day. For this is the will of My Father, that everyone who beholds the Son and believes in Him will have eternal life, and I Myself will raise him up on the last day." (6:38-40)

As the Son of God, Jesus came into this world in the flesh. He never flaunted Himself during His ministry, but He gave all glory only to God. To prevent any misconceptions from arising in the people who saw Him with their physical eyes, Jesus only shared about God, and He only did what was the will of God.

When Jesus says, "Of all that He has given Me I lose nothing," He means that He didn't have any evil in His heart and deeds that might cause anyone to turn away from God but in His love for the sinners, He gave His life to pay the penalty of their sins. And not only did He show love for all people, but with each soul He met, He took special care to keep them from going astray and tried to give them every opportunity to repent. So, when Jesus says He 'lost nothing', He means He lost no one because everyone who accepts Him and casts away sin and evil from his heart and comes into the truth becomes a child of God.

The reason Jesus came into this world was so that all people could receive eternal life and on the last day live once again. So how is a person supposed to be able to live again? When a farmer sows seed, the seed dies, but it puts forth a new sprout from it. And in the winter, trees look bare and dead, but when spring comes around, new buds begin to sprout, and the tree comes back to life. As a maggot transforms into a cicada, and a pupa transforms into a butterfly, on the last day, when the Lord returns, all people who believe in Him will transform into resurrected bodies.

As it is written in 1 Corinthians 15:52, *"The trumpet will sound, and the dead will be raised imperishable, and we will be changed,"* when the Lord returns, the bodies of the believers who had already died will resurrect and transform into imperishable, resurrected bodies, and reunite with their spirits that were in Heaven. And instantaneously, the believers who are still alive will also transform into radiant resurrected bodies and be lifted up. This is called the "Rapture".

And in these spiritual bodies, the believers will partake in the Seven-year Wedding Banquet in the air, and then return to the earth and reign with the Lord for a thousand years. After that period of time, there will be the Great White Throne Judgment, after which the eternal dwelling place in Heaven for each believer will be designated depending on the rewards they reaped.

Eating the Flesh of the Son of Man and Drinking His Blood for Eternal Life

After the fall of Southern Judah and the destruction of the Temple, the Jews needed a new congregation, and a new place to carry out their lives of faith. This is the historic background in which the Jewish synagogue was born. The synagogue was a place where all kinds of meetings were held, and it was also the resource center for a variety of different things, such as children's education, and the laws. It was in a synagogue in Capernaum that Jesus taught that He was the bread of life that came down out of heaven.

The Jews Grumble About Jesus

"Therefore the Jews were grumbling about Him,

because He said, 'I am the bread that came down out of heaven.' They were saying, 'Is not this Jesus, the son of Joseph, whose father and mother we know? How does He now say, "I have come down out of heaven"?' Jesus answered and said to them, 'Do not grumble among yourselves. No one can come to Me unless the Father who sent Me draws him; and I will raise him up on the last day. 'It is written in the prophets, "And they shall all be taught of God." Everyone who has heard and learned from the Father, comes to Me. Not that anyone has seen the Father, except the One who is from God; He has seen the Father.'" (6:41-46)

The Jews began to grumble among themselves. They were sure that Jesus was born of Mary and Joseph. They had also seen Him living with them. But since Jesus was now claiming to have come from heaven, they did not understand. However, these people were grumbling because they were looking at Jesus only with their fleshly eyes. Even though He showed that God was with Him through miraculous signs and wonders, they were blinded by their fleshly thoughts, and they did not believe.

So with a gentle tone, Jesus said to them, "Do not grumble among yourselves. No one can come to Me unless the Father who sent Me draws him." This applies to us today. If God does not watch over our minds and hearts and guide our footsteps, no one would be able to come to Jesus. Listening to the Word and understanding it is also only possible by the grace of God.

The statement, "Everyone who has heard and learned from the Father" does not mean that someone met God and learned from Him face to face. It means that when someone listens to the Word or reads it, God gives that person the enlightenment or understanding they need. In other words, someone who worships God in spirit and in truth with faith will listen to the words of the Lord's servants and receive it as if the words were coming from God Himself, he will be led to understanding. There are special cases where people actually meet God face to face, or hear His voice directly, like Moses or Elijah; but in most cases, people meet Him while studying and understanding His Word, or through visions, and the like. Even if we don't get to actually see God with our eyes, we can still meet Him and experience Him while studying the Bible, as the Holy Spirit moves us.

Let's say for example that we find out that it is the will of God to love even our enemies, and we try to forgive and love someone whom we really used to dislike. We can cast out the sin called 'hatred', and have spiritual love, with the strength of the Holy Spirit to the extent that we try. When we do this, we bear fruits of love, fruits of the Spirit, and fruits of truth—this is what it means to 'come' to Jesus and to God.

After hearing that everyone who has learned from the Father can come to Jesus, the Jews may have misunderstood and asked, "Who saw God? And when did they learn from Him?" That is why Jesus added that this does not actually mean that someone has physically 'seen' the Father.

The Bread Which I Will Give for the Life of the World is My Flesh

> "Truly, truly, I say to you, he who believes has eternal life. I am the bread of life. Your fathers ate the manna in the wilderness, and they died. This is the bread which comes down out of heaven, so that one may eat of it and not die. I am the living bread that came down out of heaven; if anyone eats of this bread, he will live forever; and the bread also which I will give for the life of the world is My flesh." (6:47-51)

Unless you pay for the price of something, you cannot gain it. Likewise, even though you know the Word of life, unless you believe in it and act according to it, you cannot gain eternal life (James 2:22). Someone who does not know God will hate, be resentful, and live his life according to his desires. On the contrary, someone who has faith will, according to God's Word, cast out envy, jealousy, and evil, and strive to live a life of joy and thanksgiving. This is because he knows and believes that he can have eternal life as long as he lives according to the Word.

The Israelites who came out of Egypt ate the manna sent by God, but with the exception of Joshua and Caleb, they all died in the desert. This is because despite the fact that they saw numerous signs and wonders, whenever they faced hardship, they were resentful and complaining, instead of showing their faith. Although they ate the manna sent by God from heaven, because they did not act in faith, they couldn't gain true life.

But Jesus says He is the bread of life, and that anyone who

eats of His flesh will not die, but live eternally. So how can we eat the flesh of someone who was here two thousand years ago? This Scripture does not mean we have to actually eat Jesus' flesh.

Just as we eat food to maintain our physical bodies, we need to eat the bread that the Lord gives us, or His 'flesh', in order to live eternally. And the Lord's 'flesh' is symbolic of God's Word. A person who listens to God's Word and lives according to it, will in the end, resurrect and live eternally; and this is why Jesus called Himself 'the bread of life'.

For My Flesh Is True Food, and My Blood is True Drink

"Then the Jews began to argue with one another, saying, 'How can this man give us His flesh to eat?' So Jesus said to them, 'Truly, truly, I say to you, unless you eat the flesh of the Son of Man and drink His blood, you have no life in yourselves. He who eats My flesh and drinks My blood has eternal life, and I will raise him up on the last day. For My flesh is true food, and My blood is true drink.'" (6:52-55)

When Jesus called His flesh the bread or life, the Jews ridiculed Him. They made a noise, asking how they can eat Jesus' flesh. If they had even a speck of goodness in their hearts that urged them to try to understand the meaning of Jesus' words, they probably would have been enlightened by the spiritual meaning of His words. However, they began to grumble and condemn just because His words didn't match with their own thoughts and opinions. Therefore, a dispute broke out.

Nonetheless, Jesus continued to teach His spiritual message. He said they had to eat the flesh of the Son of Man and drink His blood in order to have life in themselves. So what do the flesh and the blood of the Son of Man represent?

Since Jesus called Himself the 'Son', the flesh of the Son of Man is Jesus' flesh. But if you look at John 1:1, it says, *"In the beginning was the Word, and the Word was with God, and the Word was God."* And in verse 14 it says, *"And the Word became flesh, and dwelt among us, and we saw His glory, glory as of the only begotten from the Father, full of grace and truth."*

This means that Jesus came into this world in the flesh, as God's Word. So the flesh of the Son of Man is the Word of God, which is the truth itself; and eating the flesh of the Son of Man means taking in God's Word, which are recorded in the 66 books of the Bible, as spiritual food. Jesus showed us firsthand, how to do this, by acting in the truth—exactly according to God's Word—and by doing this in the midst of us, He gave us His flesh.

When we take in food, we need to wash it down with some form of liquid. Likewise, we need to take in the flesh of the Son of Man with a drink of truth, which is the blood of the Son of Man. Drinking the 'blood of the Son of Man' means to take the Words of God that one took in as spiritual food, and act upon them with faith. For example, if we learned about the command, "Pray", we should pray, edify ourselves, and try to act in the truth.

Faith is not just listening to God's Word and becoming enlightened by it. It is acting upon it and abiding by it. From James 2:26 we know that if we know the Word but don't act according to it, then we have dead faith. Dead faith cannot give us life. Therefore a life gained by eating the flesh and drinking the blood of Jesus Christ lives eternally. Jesus compared His flesh and blood to true bread and drink. He did this because just as we need daily bread to maintain life, we need to eat His flesh and drink His blood in order to live eternally.

But we cannot live according to God's Word simply with human strength alone. First, we ourselves need to have the will and the effort to try to live according to His Word. Then, we need to receive the Lord's grace and power through fervent prayer, and lastly, we need to receive the help of the Holy Spirit. If we could cast out our sins with our own strength, then Jesus had no reason to be crucified on the cross, and God has no reason to send down the Holy Spirit. Because we alone cannot solve the problem of sin, Jesus had to die on the cross to pay for the penalty of our sins and God had to send the Holy Spirit to help us live according to His Word.

Whoever Eats My Flesh and Drinks My Blood

"He who eats My flesh and drinks My blood abides

in Me, and I in him. As the living Father sent Me, and I live because of the Father, so he who eats Me, he also will live because of Me. This is the bread which came down out of heaven; not as the fathers ate and died; he who eats this bread will live forever.' These things He said in the synagogue as He taught in Capernaum." (6:56-59)

People think that when they believe in Jesus, they naturally are in Jesus, and Jesus is in them. But the Bible does not say that. It says that one must eat the flesh of the Son of Man and drink His blood. Jesus did not come to this world on His own. He was sent by God to this world. But the Jews had a problem with even the mere fact that God sent Him here. Because Jesus was clearly sent by God, as evidence, He said, "so he who eats Me, he also will live because of Me."

At the time, even the disciples couldn't understand what Jesus was saying; however, after Jesus died on the cross and resurrected, they came to understand. Then why did Jesus say things in such a spiritual manner that no one could clearly understand? It was for the people who were to come in the future. As it is written in John 14:26, *"But the Helper, the Holy Spirit, whom the Father will send in My name, He will teach you all things, and bring to your remembrance all that I said to you,"* Jesus said these things so that the people of the future who receive the Holy Spirit will read and understand these words and gain strength from them.

The Disciples
Who Left Jesus' Side

Generally, people have a tendency to believe only after seeing something firsthand with their own eyes. When someone talks about the spiritual world which cannot be seen with the physical eyes, they don't try to believe. Jesus knew that even among His disciples, there were some who, like the Jews, were mumbling to themselves because they could not understand His spiritual words. But Jesus continues to speak spiritual words to them because they would eventually see Him dying on the cross, resurrecting, and ascending into heaven

It Is the Spirit Who Gives Life; the Flesh Profits Nothing

> "Therefore many of His disciples, when they heard this said, 'This is a difficult statement; who can listen to it?' But Jesus, conscious that His disciples grumbled at this, said to them, 'Does this cause you to stumble? What then if you see the Son of Man ascending to where He was before? It is the Spirit who gives life; the flesh profits nothing; the words that I have spoken to you are spirit and are life.'" (6:60-63)

When Jesus was teaching at the meeting place in Capernaum, there were some among Jesus' disciples who were talking among themselves, saying that His teachings were hard to understand. The teachings that were difficult to grasp and hard to understand were that Jesus was 'the bread that came down out of heaven' and that one had to 'eat His flesh in order to live.' If even Jesus' disciples couldn't understand, so much for the likelihood of other people understanding!

Jesus knew the disciples' hearts very well. He was sad that He couldn't teach them about the deeper dimensions of the spiritual world. He only spoke of the truth, but it became a stumbling block. People with many stumbling blocks in their hearts have them because they have many different forms of evil inside of them. Knowing that the disciples were mumbling to themselves, Jesus asked them, "Does this cause you to stumble?" He wanted to give them the correct answer. Then He asks what they would do when they see Him dying, resurrecting, and ascending into heaven.

The Spirit is from God, and 'spirit' is unchanging, good, and true. The Spirit gives us life and ultimately leads us to eternal life. For example, obeying, praying, loving, forgiving, etc., are a sign of being in the Spirit. On the contrary, being in the flesh is not of the truth, and ultimately leads to death. Being reluctant to pray, hating, judging, condemning, etc., and having evil in the heart, as opposed to loving and forgiving, is a life in faith that is based on the flesh.

Being in the flesh causes others to misunderstand, and it causes quarrels to arise. Two people may receive the same words of correction, or reprimand, but a person of spirit will obey, change his ways and repent, whereas a person of flesh will feel angry, or harbor other unpleasant feelings in his heart. With this type of faith based on the flesh, one cannot receive eternal life. If we take in God's Word simply with our head only as knowledge and if we judge and condemn, then we are also leading a life in faith that is based on the flesh.

This does not give us life; therefore we must quickly change this to faith based on the Spirit. We need to take in God's Word not with our knowledge and thoughts, but with our hearts and the Holy Spirit. We need to open our hearts wide and with a strong "Amen!", we need to take it in as spiritual food. Even if we are deacons or elders of the church, if we lead a faith life of the flesh, when hardships come our way we cannot overcome them with true faith.

On the flip side, when in the Spirit, we can do anything. Things that seem impossible to the human mind are possible in the Spirit with faith. As the Lord said, everything can be done according to our faith. If we have spiritual faith, everything occurs according to our faith. Because of this great difference between being in the Spirit and being in the flesh, Jesus emphasized the fact that we should cast out the flesh, which profits nothing, and strive to be in the Spirit. So everything Jesus taught the disciples up until now had been spirit and life, so He deeply wanted His teachings to give life to them and lead them to eternal life.

The Disciples Leave, Unable to Understand the Spiritual Messages

"'But there are some of you who do not believe' for Jesus knew from the beginning who they were who did not believe, and who it was that would betray Him. And He was saying, 'For this reason I have said to you, that no one can come to Me unless it has been granted him from the Father.' As a result of this many of His disciples withdrew and were not walking with Him anymore." (6:64-66)

It's only natural that the Jews could not understand Jesus' spiritual messages. But even His disciples, who had spent a long time with Him, could not understand and could not believe His messages either. They understood them after Jesus' resurrection, but at the time, they just could not understand. Jesus already knew that among them, Judas Iscariot would not believe even until the very end. That is why He talked about the one who would betray Him; and unfortunately, that's exactly what Judas did. He sold his teacher and went the way of death.

The people who followed Him hoping for more signs such as the sign of the two fish and five loaves also did not understand the spiritual messages, and they too finally left Jesus' side. That is why Jesus said no one can come to Him unless God grants it. This still applies today. Occasionally, there are people who cannot live in the truth, and then end up leaving the church. Because the Word of God delivered from the altar become like a sharp-edged sword that pierces the soul and spirit, separates the joints, and divides the bone and marrow, there are people who are unable to withstand it, and leave. However, if they truly know that there is eternal life and salvation in God's Word, they would not leave.

To Whom Shall We Go? You Have Words of Eternal Life

"So Jesus said to the twelve, 'You do not want to go away also, do you?' Simon Peter answered Him, 'Lord, to whom shall we go? You have words of eternal life. We have believed and have come to know that You are the Holy One of God.' Jesus answered them, 'Did I Myself not choose you, the twelve, and yet one of you is a devil?' Now He meant Judas the son of Simon Iscariot, for he, one of the twelve, was going to betray Him." (6:67-71)

After Jesus performed signs and wonders, many people wanted to become His disciples and followed Him. But because they could not understand His spiritual messages, one by one, they began to leave. Jesus was different from the kind of Messiah they had in mind. How do you think Jesus felt, as He looked on at these people?

So Jesus asked the twelve disciples, "You do not want to go away also, do you?" Peter, who usually likes to be very involved, made a surprising confession saying, "Lord, to whom shall we go? You have words of eternal life. We have believed and have come to know that You are the Holy One of God."

Like a big brother, Peter was always in the forefront. Whenever Jesus and His disciples went somewhere, Peter was there guiding and leading everyone else. But even Peter, who confessed that Jesus is the Holy One of God, and that he would never leave His side, on the night that Jesus was arrested, he denied Him three times. Peter didn't have it in his heart to do that, but because it was before he received the Holy Spirit, and his flesh was still weak, he had taken on that kind of reaction before he knew it.

Jesus also knew that among the twelve disciples He had chosen, there was one who would turn Him in for money. This is where we need to be careful. Just because a person spent time with Jesus, listened to His Words, and saw the wonders He performed, that does not mean he has salvation.

When Judas Iscariot first became Jesus' disciple, he probably never imagined that he would betray his teacher for money. He did not put into action the Words of truth he learned from Jesus; instead, he began to sin little by little by stealing money from the treasury. Because he was giving into Satan's temptations and sinning, Jesus said, "yet one of you is a devil." This is why we shouldn't stop at just knowing God's Word; we need to take in the flesh of the Son of Man, drink His blood, live in the truth, and thereby walk toward eternal life.

Chapter 7

The Teaching
at the Feast of Tabernacles

Jesus Goes to Jerusalem
in Secret

Basing His ministry in Galilee, Jesus ministered mainly in the northern areas of Israel, like Capernaum and Bethsaida. These areas had a strong presence of people from gentile nations; so the people in these parts did not really ostracize or persecute Jesus. However, the people in the southern parts of the region of Judea, typically around Jerusalem, persecuted Jesus to the point of trying to kill Him.

As the Feast of Tabernacles Drew Near

"After these things Jesus was walking in Galilee, for He was unwilling to walk in Judea because the Jews were seeking to kill Him. Now the feast of the Jews, the

Feast of Booths, was near." (John 7:1-2)

The Jews had great national pride and they were confident that they were obeying God's every command. But because Jesus reprimanded and pinpointed the faults of the Pharisees and Sadducees, who were the political and religious leaders of the time, the Jews didn't have very good feelings about Jesus. And because Jesus was calling Himself the Son of God, they thought He was being blasphemous. Jesus tried to enlighten these people with the true Word of God. However, from time to time, He wisely avoided them.

Of course avoiding someone altogether without proper reason is not God's will. For example, in the case of the apostle Paul he knew if he went to Jerusalem the Jews would arrest him. But, he went anyway because it was God's will. In order to abide by God's Word, Daniel and his friends did not compromise to their environment, even if it meant being thrown into the lion's den or the fiery furnace. In this same way, if we know something is God's will, we should be able to carry out His will without even fear of death. And then there are times in the midst of carrying out God's will, when we need to wisely avoid something or someone.

When Saul was coming to kill David, in order to save himself, David once had to act like a crazy man in front of Achish, the King of Gath. This was because he couldn't risk losing his life before God's appointed time. Jesus also acted wisely, and avoided certain confrontations from time to time in order to carry out God's will at the appointed time.

Around this time, the Jewish Feast of Tabernacles was near.

The Feast of Tabernacles is also known as "Sukkoth", and it is a celebration at the end of the harvest time when the Jewish people set up tents and give thanks to God in remembrance of their ancestors' exodus out of Egypt. During this celebration, people give thanks and commemorate how God saved the Israelites from the bondage of slavery in Egypt. They also remember how God always guided and protected them in the wilderness. The Israelites kept this feast sacred by offering up bulls or rams as sacrifices every day for seven days. This is a tradition that would go on for many generations.

Jesus' Brothers Urge Him

"Therefore His brothers said to Him, 'Leave here and go into Judea, so that Your disciples also may see Your works which You are doing. For no one does anything in secret when he himself seeks to be known publicly. If You do these things, show Yourself to the world.' For not even His brothers were believing in Him." (7:3-5)

To celebrate the Feast of Tabernacles, people normally go up to the Temple of Jerusalem. As the Feast of Tabernacles drew near, and Jesus didn't look like He was planned to leave for Jerusalem, His brothers became downhearted. They wanted Jesus to go to Jerusalem and perform a sign, and then go to Judea to rally up the people's support. "Leave here and go into Judea, so that Your disciples also may see Your works which You are doing."

Jesus' brothers were urging Him to gain some publicity, since His ministry was for the good of many people. They advise Him, "For no one does anything in secret when he himself seeks to be known publicly." This may sound like a reasonable advice, and it may even seem like a good advice. However, as it is written, *"The plans of the heart belong to man, but the answer of the tongue is from the LORD"* (Proverbs 16:1), no matter how right a person's thought or idea may be, if it does not agree with God's will, it has nothing to do with God.

A good example of someone who experienced this was King Saul, Israel's first king. God told Saul to destroy everything that belonged to the Amalekites, but Saul disobeyed. He captured the enemy King, and he brought back their choice cattle and sheep. Saul reasoned that it would be well to offer up to God cattle and sheep of good quality, and he did as he pleased. His outward reason for bringing the animals was to make sacrifice to God; but in his heart, he had a desire to show his great deed to his people and win their praise. So in the end, because Saul repeatedly disobeyed Him, and refused to change his ways, God decided to disown him.

Likewise, because their own thoughts preceded God's will, Jesus' brothers grew impatient with Jesus because He was always waiting for God's set time. This was ultimately due to their lack of faith in Jesus. If Jesus' brothers had even a fundamental level of trust in Jesus and knew that Jesus' only will was to accomplish God's will in everything He did, they would not have spoken that way. Instead of commenting on what they saw right before their eyes, they probably would have tried to understand the spiritual meaning in everything Jesus did.

When you trust Jesus enough to obey whatever He says to do without questioning Him, that is when you begin to see with understanding. At the wedding in Cana, the Virgin Mary told the servants to do whatever Jesus told them to do, because she knew who Jesus was. This means that certainly, Mary must have taught her children about Jesus. However, they did not believe in Him. They began to believe only after Jesus resurrected and ascended into Heaven.

Jesus Answers, Knowing His Time

"So Jesus said to them, 'My time is not yet here, but your time is always opportune. The world cannot hate you, but it hates Me because I testify of it, that its deeds are evil. Go up to the feast yourselves; I do not go up to this feast because My time has not yet fully come.' Having said these things to them, He stayed in Galilee." (7:6-9)

When His brothers urged Him to make Himself more publically known, Jesus answered, "My time has not yet fully come." At first, His answer seems very random. However, there is a reason why Jesus answered them this way. As it is written in Ecclesiastes 3:1, *"There is an appointed time for everything. And there is a time for every event under heaven,"* there was a certain time when Jesus had to show Himself to be captured, in order to fulfill God's will. If His brothers had faith, Jesus probably would have explained all this in more detail, but because they didn't have faith, He refrained from explaining to them with much detail.

Even though Jesus only did good deeds to salvage those people who were walking toward eternal death, the world hated Him. Because Jesus was spreading the Words of light and the Words of goodness in a world under the authority of the enemy devil who has control over darkness, He was not welcomed.

Moreover, since Jesus was pointing out the evils and teaching the ways of goodness, evil people felt pierced in their hearts. Not only were the evils inside of them being displayed in broad daylight; but they couldn't show God's glory like Jesus did. It's no wonder that they were jealous of Jesus and even hated Him. And Jesus knew it was not yet time for Him to appear before men like these. That is why He told His brothers to go up to the temple before Him while He Himself stayed in Galilee.

Jesus Goes Up to Jerusalem In Secret

"But when His brothers had gone up to the feast, then He Himself also went up, not publicly, but as if, in secret. So the Jews were seeking Him at the feast and were saying, 'Where is He?' There was much grumbling among the crowds concerning Him; some were saying, 'He is a good man'; others were saying, 'No, on the contrary, He leads the people astray.' Yet no one was speaking openly of Him for fear of the Jews." (7:10-13)

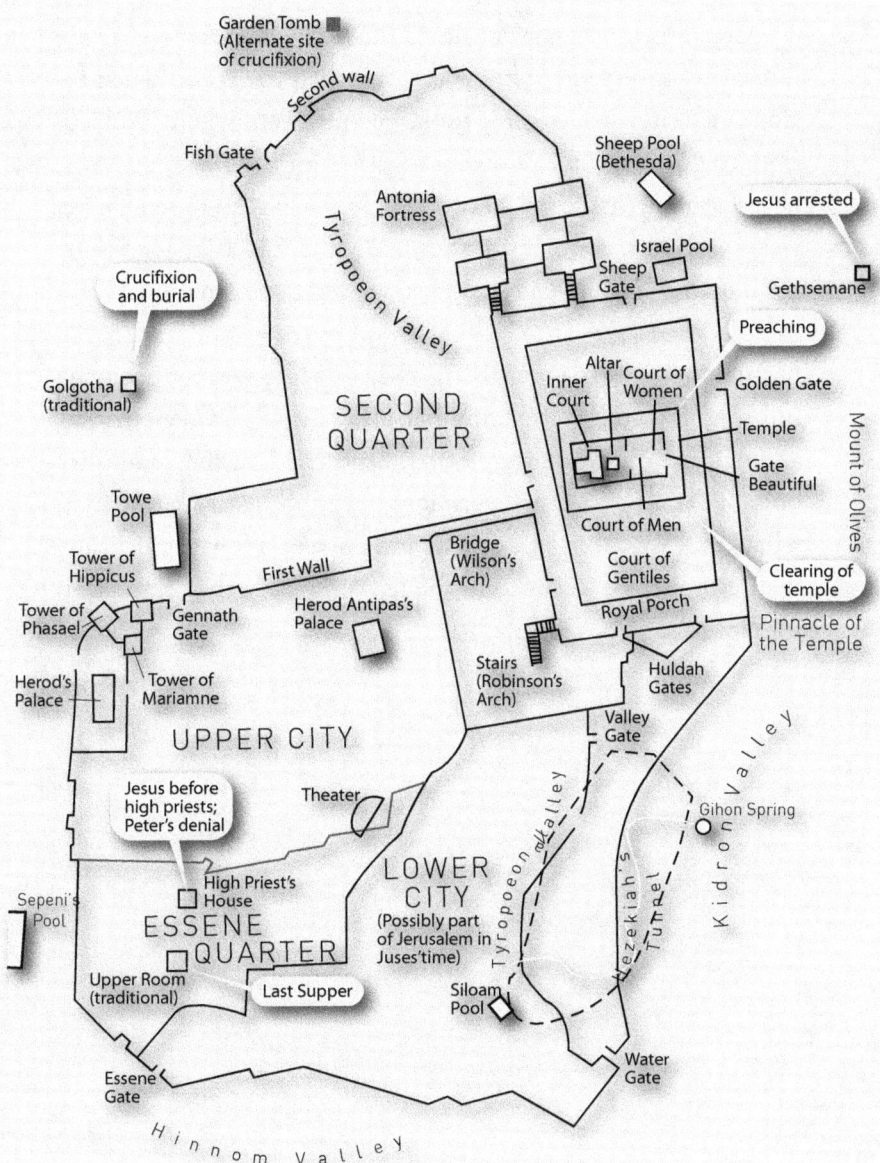

Garden Tomb
(Alternate site
of crucifixion)

Second wall

Fish Gate

Sheep Pool
(Bethesda)

Jesus arrested

Antonia
Fortress

Israel Pool

Sheep
Gate

Gethsemane

Tyropoeon Valley

Preaching

Crucifixion
and burial

Inner
Court

Altar

Court of
Women

Golden Gate

Golgotha
(traditional)

SECOND
QUARTER

Temple

Gate
Beautiful

Mount of Olives

Towe
Pool

Bridge
(Wilson's
Arch)

Court of Men

Court of
Gentiles

Clearing of
temple

Tower of
Hippicus

First Wall

Herod Antipas's
Palace

Royal Porch

Pinnacle of
the Temple

Tower of
Phasael

Gennath
Gate

Stairs
(Robinson's
Arch)

Huldah
Gates

Herod's
Palace

Tower of
Mariamne

Valley
Gate

UPPER CITY

Theater

Jesus before
high priests;
Peter's denial

LOWER
CITY
(Possibly part
of Jerusalem in
Juses' time)

Gihon Spring

Tyropoeon Valley

Hezekiah's Tunnel

Kidron Valley

Sepeni's
Pool

High Priest's
House

ESSENE
QUARTER

Upper Room
(traditional)

Last Supper

Siloam
Pool

Essene
Gate

Water
Gate

Hinnom Valley

:: Jerusalem in the New Testament Times

After His brothers went up to the temple, Jesus went up to Jerusalem in secret. He knew exactly when to go and when to stop, and with each step He took, He only went where God led Him to go. As people crowded together for the Feast, the Jews began looking for Jesus. They knew He would be there. There was much talk about Him. Some people said that He was a good man and some said that He deceived the people.

Because Jesus was doing things that were humanly impossible there were some people who were very curious about Him. Yet there were others who tried all they could to be a hindrance to Him. People with good hearts knew that what Jesus was doing was good and correct. However, fearing that Jesus may be wronged by the Jewish society, they could not speak publicly about Him.

Jesus Reveals Himself at the Temple

Befitting each situation, Jesus taught the gospel in many different ways. Sometimes He taught up in the mountains, sometimes in open fields, and other times He stood in a boat floating on the water and spoke to the people standing on the beach. At times He visited people privately in their homes, and other times He shared God's Word at the temple. There were times when He revealed teachings to just a select few of His disciples in secret.

My Teaching Is of Him Who Sent Me

"But when it was now the midst of the feast Jesus went up into the temple, and began to teach. The

Jews then were astonished, saying, 'How has this man become learned, having never been educated? So Jesus answered them and said, 'My teaching is not Mine, but His who sent Me. If anyone is willing to do His will, he will know of the teaching, whether it is of God or whether I speak from Myself. He who speaks from himself seeks his own glory; but He who is seeking the glory of the One who sent Him, He is true, and there is no unrighteousness in Him.'" (7:14-18)

When they were about halfway through the seven days of the Feast of Tabernacles, Jesus went up to the temple and taught the people there. Because Jesus taught the Bible and the Words of God with such ease, the Jews were amazed. They were amazed at Jesus' teaching because Jesus spoke the Words of God with more power than the Rabbis, who were experts of the Law. And though He had never received proper education in the Law, Jesus was freely using the Words of the Bible to precisely explain God's will. It was no wonder the people were astonished!

Standing before the people who were astounded by His teachings, Jesus gave all the glory to God. And even though He was God's Son, having the humility of a servant, He confessed that all His teachings came from God. He also stated that when people believe in the teachings and act according to them, they will know whether His teachings came from God or not. With that, He left no room for dispute.

Though words are spoken through the lips of a man, if God has control over his affairs then amazing things happen as a result of those words. Even today, if we receive the words of a servant of God with whom God truly abides, and believe in those words and obey the words as if they were the very words of God, then we can experience amazing things. In accordance with Hebrews 4:12 we know that God's Word is living and active. Therefore anyone who believes and obeys His Word will experience His power. Because God secures the words of His trusted servants, through their prayers, diseases are cured, families gain peace, non-believers receive the gospel, and many other blessings such as these come from the Father.

People who seek to gain their own glory will do whatever they can to show off their good deeds and receive compliments. Blinded by their self-interest, they step on other people and condemn them, and they act with unrighteousness. Therefore their final results are not very good. For example, Hitler, the notorious war criminal of World War II, made his people salute, "Heil Hitler!" meaning, "Hail Hitler", or "Long live Hitler!" Ultimately, Hitler and Germany both came to ruins together.

On the contrary, a person who is sent by God and seeking God's glory will bring grace to many people and save many souls. The apostle Paul dedicated his whole life for God's glory. Performing great miracles, he gave glory to God, and as the apostle of the Gentiles, he led countless souls to Christ. He devoted all of his heart and will to the cause for Christ. That's why he could boldly say, *"Be imitators of me"* (1 Corinthians 11:1). He wasn't saying this to flaunt himself; rather, he was telling people to imitate the life of Christ, as he did.

Jesus also only sought to glorify God. He never tried to

lift Himself up, or gain something for Himself. That's why when He performed the miracle of the two fish and five loaves of bread, He looked toward Heaven while blessing the food (Mark 6:41). When raising Lazarus back to life, He first lifted up a prayer giving glory to God. He became a tool to show the world the living God and His will. And, God received glory by securing every word that came out of the mouth of Jesus.

Why Do You Seek to Kill Me?

"'Did not Moses give you the Law, and yet none of you carries out the Law? Why do you seek to kill Me?' The crowd answered, 'You have a demon! Who seeks to kill You?' Jesus answered them, 'I did one deed, and you all marvel.'" (7:19-21)

In the laws which Moses received at Mount Sinai during the Exodus, there are commandments among which are, "Honor your father and your mother, you shall not murder, you shall not commit adultery, and you shall not bear false witness." The core meaning of these laws is to understand, to forgive, and to love all people with mercy and compassion.

However, the Jews at the time were busy using the laws as they saw fit to condemn people, even to the point of criticizing Jesus for His good deeds. When Jesus cured a man who had been invalid for 38 years, they tried to kill Him because He did this on the Sabbath day. If a sign occurs, and God is glorified, they should be rejoicing. But instead, they tried to kill Jesus claiming He broke the Sabbath.

Seeing their evil hearts, Jesus said to them, "And yet none of you carries out the Law? Why do you seek to kill Me?" He was teaching them that although God gave them the laws to do good deeds, they were using it to try to kill someone. A person who carries out the law correctly would never do something like that.

The Jews could not understand the spiritual meaning of Jesus' words, and they accused Him of being possessed of demon. The Jews considered Jesus to be delusional about the notion that He was being persecuted and victimized. Although they never openly tried to kill Him, in reality, within their hearts they already had the desire to kill Him (John 5:18). This conversation openly displayed the evil inside their hearts. Not knowing why Jesus said what He said, they were simply accusing Him of being demon-possessed, according to their own judgment.

The Jews could not understand why Jesus had healed the sick on the Sabbath day, and so they judged Him and considered Him somewhat strange. So by reminding them how they themselves permit performing circumcision on the Sabbath day, Jesus provided them an important lesson.

If A Man Receives Circumcision on the Sabbath

"For this reason Moses has given you circumcision (not because it is from Moses, but from the fathers), and on the Sabbath you circumcise a man. If a man receives circumcision on the Sabbath so that the Law of Moses will not be broken, are you angry with Me because I made an entire man well on the Sabbath? Do not judge according to appearance, but judge with righteous judgment." (7:22-24)

Circumcision is a ritual of the Israelites in which the foreskin of the penis is removed from a male baby 8 days after birth. This practice began from the time of Abraham, the father of faith (Genesis 17:10-14). After making His covenant of blessing with Abraham, God told Abraham to circumcise his whole family as a sign of receiving the covenant. If someone did not receive circumcision, he was cut off from God's people, and he could not receive the promised blessing.

Even Moses, who took on the great task of the Exodus, was almost put to death by God because he hadn't circumcised himself. Because as the leader in charge of such an important mission as leading the Israelites out of Egypt, Moses had to be more perfect and whole than anyone else. God sternly warned Moses of the importance of circumcision. The Jews considered Moses' experience as a great lesson and kept in mind the very importance of circumcision. That is why, in the Jewish society of Jesus' time, even after 2,000 years after Abraham's covenant, performing circumcision was permitted without reservation, even on the Sabbath day.

So Jesus said to these Jews who had judged and condemned His actions, "If a man receives circumcision on the Sabbath so that the Law of Moses will not be broken, are you angry with Me because I made an entire man well on the Sabbath?" Jesus did not say this because He could not understand the Jews' sensitivity to His healing the sick on the Sabbath, or because He was frustrated with them. Using circumcision as an illustration, He just wanted to teach them what was right. Telling them that love and compassion must go before the laws, He taught them, "Do not judge according to appearance, but judge with righteous judgment."

In 1 Samuel 16:7, when Samuel tried to anoint Jesse's first-born son, Eliab, God says to him, *"The LORD does not look at the things man looks at. Man looks at the outward appearance, but the LORD looks at the heart."* Jesus, who knows God's heart very well, also looks at the center of man's heart, and not his outward appearance (James 2:1-4). That is why He was trying to teach the Jews, who were judging and condemning with the laws, to judge with truth and justice instead.

People Who Judge Based On Appearance

"So some of the people of Jerusalem were saying, 'Is this not the man whom they are seeking to kill?' Look, He is speaking publicly, and they are saying nothing to Him. The rulers do not really know that this is the Christ, do they? However, we know where this man is from; but whenever the Christ may come, no one knows where He is from." (7:25-27)

When Jesus asked the crowd, "Why do you try to kill Me?"

the Jews realized that their inner motives had been uncovered, so they began accusing Jesus of being demon-possessed, and treated Him as if He was speaking in delirium. Then a third party appeared and testified to this truth. Some people came and said that the leaders were trying to kill Jesus. And so, the truthfulness of Jesus' Words was confirmed by the third party.

Because God is a God of justice, when we walk the path of righteousness, He makes sure that truth always prevails (Psalm 37:6; Amos 5:24). Therefore a mature Christian will not argue or quarrel, even if he is falsely accused or is treated unfairly. This is because when the time comes, all things will be revealed.

However, the third party that validated Jesus' Words was no different from the people who tried to capture Jesus. They were inquiring why the accused had not been promptly taken into custody yet. Just as the whole world looks blue when one looks at it through blue sunglasses, these people were looking at Jesus with negative emotions and thoughts, so they could only see reasons to condemn Him.

Likewise, when you listen to God's Word with a good and true heart, you become inspired and moved to repent and change. However, when you mix your own emotions or thoughts, saying things like, "It probably went like this, or like that," then you will ultimately commit the grave sin of judging and condemning.

The crowd of people also asked, "Do the rulers know that this person is the Christ?" And then they added, "But we know where this man is from." What they meant was that they knew Jesus was born as Joseph's son, meaning that He is not a god, and that He is not God's son. According to their logic and reasoning, no one should know where the Messiah comes from.

But is it true that no one could have known where the Messiah came from? The Bible does not record the exact date and time of Christ's, or the Messiah's birth. At the time, it was not easy for either the teachers of the law or the Sadducees to predict the time of the Messiah's birth, because they only had a couple verses that referred to His birth (Daniel 9:25; Malachi 3:1). Therefore there were differing opinions even among them about the Messiah's birth. They even thought that the Messiah will have a supernatural and occult personality, and that He would appear in a sudden manner. However, even though it might have been hard to know the exact time of the Messiah's birth, there are plenty of prophecies that tell us about the Messiah.

Micah 5:2 reads, *"But as for you, Bethlehem Ephrathah, too little to be among the clans of Judah, from you One will go forth for Me to be ruler in Israel. His goings forth are from long ago, from the days of eternity."* Just as this prophecy stated, Jesus was born in Bethlehem, into the family of Judah.

The fact that the Messiah would be born in Bethlehem was known even among the Jews living in Jesus' time. If you look at Matthew 2:1-6, it says that after hearing from the three wise men that a king was born, King Herod wanted to kill him, because he was afraid of losing his position as king. So he gathered all the chief priests and scribes and asked them, "Where is the Christ supposed to be born?" Then, using the prophecy in the book of Micah, they answered that He would be born in Bethlehem, in the land of Judea.

Deuteronomy 18:18 talks about how Jesus will be considered a prophet, and Isaiah 9:1 prophesies that Jesus' public ministry will begin in Galilee. There are many other prophecies throughout the Bible, like Isaiah 53, where prophecies about Jesus can be found. However, even without the prophecies, we can decipher the true Messiah by the powerful works of God that He performed, and by the words that came out of His mouth.

Also, the lonely and pious Simon, Anna (the woman who spent her whole life praying in the temple and waiting for the Messiah), the good shepherds who were tending the sheep, and the three wise men all recognized the Messiah (Luke 2; Matthew 2:1-11). Either guided by the Holy Spirit, or notified by the angels, these people went to baby Jesus and worshipped Him, giving glory to God. Therefore the people who confessed that no one should know where the Messiah comes from, were actually confessing that they are not people of God. The Messiah was right before their eyes, and still they were not able to recognize Him.

I Have Not Come Of Myself

"Then Jesus cried out in the temple, teaching and saying, 'You both know Me and know where I am from; and I have not come of Myself, but He who sent Me is true, whom you do not know. I know Him, because I am from Him, and He sent Me.' So they were seeking to seize Him; and no man laid his hand on Him, because His hour had not yet come. But many of the crowd believed in Him; and they were saying, 'When the Christ comes, He will not perform more signs than those which this man has, will He?'" (7:28-31)

The Jews knew Jesus' birthplace and His family situation, but that was only a physical aspect of Jesus. So Jesus first acknowledged their words, and then He told them that He came from God.

He first said to them, "You both know Me and know where I am from." Here, the word 'know' has two meanings. A person who understands Jesus' words in spirit and believes that He is the true Christ, knows that He came to this world as God's Son and the Savior. On the other hand, a person who understands His Words literally and in the flesh knows that Jesus is the son of Joseph, the carpenter. So when the Jews said they 'knew' Jesus, the literal meaning is what they meant.

Jesus said He did not come by Himself, and that there is He who sent Him. Then He added that the One who sent Him is true. When Jesus says He did not come by Himself, it means that He came from the Father God. Under God's providence, Jesus, who was with God from the beginning, came to this world to save mankind, whose death due to sin was inevitable.

Jesus also said, "He who sent Me is true." Truth means spirit, life, and that which is eternal—never decaying or changing. And the power of the true God, who is truth, was with Him thus far, which is how so many signs and wonders occurred through Jesus.

Jesus said that He knew the One they did not know. Many people interact with the president through all kinds of different media, and they claim, "I know the president." However, this does not mean that the president knows them all. The president must also claim to know someone, in order for him to say he really knows the president. The same goes for knowing God. If someone claims to know God, he must have a relationship with God. Having a relationship with God means living in the light, or living according to God's Word (1 John 1:7). But the Jews did not have this kind of relationship with God. They had never even seen an image of God. Furthermore, they were men of flesh, so they needed to see everything with their physical eyes. This is why Jesus said they do not know God. Then He explained that He knows God because He is from God, and that He came to this world according to God's will.

Then the people in the temple who were listening to this began to show mixed reactions. Some people said Jesus was blaspheming God, and they tried to seize Him. Fortunately, it was not His appointed time yet, so they could not do anything to Him. On the contrary, there were many who looked at Jesus in a positive light. He did not just simply say, "I am the truth, so believe in Me." He led the people to believe by performing signs and wonders to prove God was with Him.

Beginning with a man who was sick for 38 years, Jesus healed people of all kinds of diseases. He healed the blind and the deaf, and made them whole again. He turned water into wine, fed over five thousand people with two fish and five barley loaves, and He walked on water too. Many people either heard about these signs or witnessed them first-hand. That is why they asked, "When the Christ comes, He will not perform more signs than those which this man has, will He?" Even though they did not witness exactly what happened, the people with good hearts looked on at the things that Jesus did and affirmed it as the truth.

The Jews Try to Capture Jesus

After seeing Jesus performing great signs, the people glorified God, saying that a great prophet has appeared among them, and that God has come to save His people (Luke 7:16). However, not everyone thought this way. There were those Jews who wanted to capture Jesus.

The Chief Priests and the Pharisees

"The Pharisees heard the crowd muttering these things about Him, and the chief priests and the Pharisees sent officers to seize Him. Therefore Jesus said, 'For a little while longer I am with you, then I go to Him who sent Me. You will seek Me, and will not find Me; and where I am, you cannot come.' The Jews then said to one another, 'Where does this man intend to go that we will not find Him? He is not intending to go to the Dispersion among the Greeks, and teach the Greeks, is He? What is this statement that He said, 'You will seek Me, and will not find Me; and where I am, you cannot come.'? " (7:32-36)

The chief priests and the Pharisees took notice of the people's great interest in Jesus, and all the talk that was going on about Him. As the head of the priests, once a year, the High Priest is in charge of going into the Holy of Holies set apart as holy, and makes a sacrifice for the people. And as a religious leader, he has the right to exercise political power. As priests and being who they were, they could no longer just observe as Jesus proclaimed that He was sent by God. So finally, they plotted with the Pharisees to capture Jesus, and they sent out their guards after Him.

In this dire situation, Jesus boldly told the people that He would be returning to the Father God. He explained that He would no longer be here on earth, and that at God's appointed time, He would take up the cross, resurrect, and sit on the right hand of God. But not understanding the spiritual meaning of Jesus' words, the Jews including the Pharisees and scribes ridiculed Him.

The Pharisees were one of the major Jewish divisions that came about between the first century B.C. and the first century A.D. The Pharisees believed in the existence of angels, the resurrection of the dead, and strived for strict adherence to the laws of Judaism, down to the last clause. However, Jesus reprimanded these people, saying, *"Woe to you, scribes and Pharisees, hypocrites... "* (Matthew 23:13). He did this because like whitewashed tombs, they appeared holy on the outside, but they were filled with evil inside their hearts.

Scribes are those people who interpret and teach the laws. Since the time the Jewish captives returned from Babylon, they began a vigorous movement to keep the laws enshrined within the state of Judea. So from then on, the teachers who could interpret the laws and teach the people how to apply the laws took on a very important task. But because these teachers boasted of their authority, basing their reason on the tradition of the elders—which came from the passing down of the laws by mouth—they couldn't avoid the conflict they had with Jesus, who only interpreted the Bible according to God's will. On top of that, Jesus' powerful Words put their power and authority at risk.

These Jews could not understand Jesus, and they continued to incorporate their fleshly thoughts to interpret Jesus' Words. They wondered, "If He says we won't be able to find Him, even though we tried, does this mean that He is planning to leave this place and go to the Greeks?" Jesus never said He was going to Greece, and He never had intentions of doing so, but they were making all kinds of wrong assumptions.

Why did these people, who supposedly studied and taught God's Word, have such a hard time understanding Jesus'

Words? Being of the flesh, they incorporated their worldly wisdom and knowledge into everything. They also considered their own knowledge, thoughts, and experiences to be better than everyone else's. That is why they could not meet God, who is spirit (Romans 8:5-8). Because they were fixated on thoughts of the flesh, which are hostile to God, they did not recognize who Jesus was.

Jesus' Promise of the Holy Spirit

"Now on the last day, the great day of the feast, Jesus stood and cried out, saying, 'If anyone is thirsty, let him come to Me and drink.' 'He who believes in Me', as the Scripture said, 'from his innermost being will flow rivers of living water.' But this He spoke of the Spirit, whom those who believed in Him were to receive; for the Spirit was not yet given, because Jesus was not yet glorified." (7:37-39)

For a man walking through a desert where the sun is scorching down hard, one drink of cold water is more precious than a bag of gold. But this is no more than mere thirst of the flesh. In all human beings, there is another type of thirst: spiritual thirst. This is the type of thirst that Jesus was talking about.

There are also two types of spiritual thirst. One type is a thirst that an evil person feels. An evil person continually seeks evil. These types of people never have peace during their lifetime. Israel's first king, King Saul, was a very humble person before he became king. However, after becoming king, he became proud and stubborn, and disobeyed God. He was always anxious and worried about losing his throne to David, whom God recognized as "The one after My heart." As a result, Saul spent his whole life trying to kill David. With his own evil heart, he inflicted hardship on himself, and he suffered from burning anguish in his heart.

However, the type of thirst that a good person feels is totally contrary to this. A lonely person has a strong desire to meet a true friend, with whom he can build an unchanging relationship and with whom he can share his deepest thoughts and feelings. Parents and children, and husbands and wives, all want to have a trusting relationship with one another. Everyone has thirsts in his inner being for love, faith, truth, joy, and companionship.

After celebrating the Feast of Tabernacles in Jerusalem, Jesus said to the people who were feeling this type of thirst, "If anyone is thirsty, let him come to Me and drink." Jesus says then, rivers of living water will flow from their innermost being. Here, the living water signifies the Holy Spirit that the believers in Christ receive. For those who accept Jesus and receive the Holy Spirit, their hunger for righteousness is satiated, and the thirst of their soul is quenched. That is why the Scripture said, "From his innermost being will flow rivers of living water."

Jesus Becomes the Center of Controversy

"Some of the people therefore, when they heard these words, were saying, 'This certainly is the Prophet.' Others were saying, 'This is the Christ.' Still others were saying, 'Surely the Christ is not going to come from Galilee, is He? Has not the Scripture said that the Christ comes from the descendants of David, and from Bethlehem, the village where David was?' So a division occurred in the crowd because of Him. Some of them wanted to seize Him, but no one laid hands on Him." (7:40-44)

Everyone had different opinions about Jesus. Some said He was a "prophet", others said He was the "Christ", and still others doubted, "How can the Christ come from Galilee?"

Why would the people's thoughts be so different? This is because some saw Jesus from a spiritual viewpoint, and some saw Him through the window of their own mind's framework. The people who saw Him with their spiritual eyes accepted Jesus as the Christ, but those who saw Him based on their knowledge couldn't see Jesus for who He truly was. They ended up doubting Him. That is why, based on their historical knowledge or background, they questioned, "Surely the Christ is not going to come from Galilee, is He?"

As the most northern region of Israel, Galilee was often vulnerable to the invasion of many foreign nations. Therefore Galilee had a strong presence of gentile cultures. That is why in

Isaiah 9:1, it is called, "Galilee of the Gentiles", and in John 7:52, the Pharisees said, *"Search, and see that no prophet arises out of Galilee."* According to the framework of their knowledge and logic, they believe that there is no way the Christ, who is to save Israel, could be born in such a lowly place. Since they were comparing Jesus to an image of the Messiah which they created, based on their own knowledge, they could not grasp the truth.

At the time, the Israelites were under the suppression of the Romans, so they dreamed of a Messiah with political and military power who could save them from the Romans. Jesus did not meet their expectations. In their eyes, He was no more than the son of a poor carpenter. That is why they couldn't possibly see Him as the king who would save all of Israel.

So based upon the Scripture, "The Christ will come from Bethlehem", they did not acknowledge Jesus. They actually used the prophecy recorded in the Bible about the Messiah to deny Jesus.

Yes, just as the prophecy said, Jesus was born in Bethlehem, and then He grew up in Nazareth. But the people only knew Him as a Nazarene. Since they looked on with their predisposed thoughts, they couldn't see the truth. As a result of these differing viewpoints, a controversy arose. Among these people, there were some who tried to find a reason to capture Jesus; however, it was not God's appointed time yet, so no one could lay their hands on Him.

Why Did You Not Bring Him In?

"The officers then came to the chief priests and
Pharisees, and they said to them, 'Why did you not
bring Him?' The officers answered, 'Never has a man
spoken the way this man speaks.' The Pharisees then
answered them, 'You have not also been led astray, have
you? No one of the rulers or Pharisees has believed in
Him, has he? But this crowd which does not know the
Law is accursed.'" (7:45-49)

When the officers sent by the chief priests and Pharisees
heard Jesus' words, they noticed He wasn't like anyone else,
and they felt power and authority in His words. And because
Jesus was perfect in all His ways, even though their masters
commanded them to capture Him, the officers had to return
without capturing Him. To their servants who came back
empty-handed, the chief priests and Pharisees asked, "Why did
you not bring Him?"

To their frustrated masters, the officers made an unexpected
reply, "Never has a man spoken the way this man speaks." From
the officers' standpoint, there was always a crowd of people
around Jesus, so it was not easy to capture Him. They could have
used this, and many other excuses for not being able to capture
Jesus, but they answered their masters rather boldly. This shows
that these officers were strongly moved by Jesus' words.

After hearing the officers' report, the Pharisees rebuked them
harshly in an inflated tone, "You have not also been led astray,
have you?" Then they asked if any of the rulers or the Pharisees,

who were supposedly among the elite, had also been led astray. We must understand that these people were full of pride about their status, and they considered themselves different from the uneducated, common people. They thought that if any one of the rulers or Pharisees believed in Jesus, then that meant that he had been led astray, and that he is a preposterous person who doesn't know the laws.

That is why the Pharisees didn't refrain from judging those people who followed Jesus and called them "accursed". They were judging them, using the words from Deuteronomy 27:26, *"'Cursed is he who does not confirm the words of this law by doing them.' And all the people shall say, 'Amen.'"* The very people who took pride in knowing the laws were actually distorting God's Words.

The Pharisees were assiduous. Not only did they divide up the laws into small sections to obey them more accurately, but they even diligently memorized and researched old interpretations of the laws that had been handed down by word of mouth. So when they saw people who had viewpoints that were even slightly different from their own, they condemned them as foolish, and even cursed them.

But who are the people who are truly cursed? It was the closed-minded and haughty Pharisees who were walking toward the way of death by refusing to believe in Jesus. After killing Jesus, they received upon themselves, and their generations thereafter, the curse of paying back the price for Jesus' blood. In 70 A.D., after the fall of Jerusalem, the Jews were chased from their homeland and scattered all over the world. And for a long time after that, they were persecuted and oppressed by many other nations.

In Romans 12:14, it says, *"Bless those who persecute you; bless and do not curse."* A person with a good heart that is filled with the truth will never hurt anyone with his words, or expose another person's shortcomings. He will not have evil thoughts, and will not be pleased with unrighteousness. Instead, he will only allow good and beautiful words to come out of his mouth. Jesus had the power and authority to judge the world; however, He never cursed anyone indiscriminately as the Pharisees did.

Nicodemus Defends Jesus

"Nicodemus (he who came to Him before, being one of them) said to them, 'Our Law does not judge a man unless it first hears from him and knows what he is doing, does it?' They answered him, 'You are not also from Galilee, are you? Search, and see that no prophet arises out of Galilee.' Everyone went to his home."
(7:50-53)

When the Pharisees continued to curse those who believed in Jesus, Nicodemus could not just look on any longer, and he pointed out their unjust and prejudiced views. Nicodemus questioned, "Our Law does not judge a man unless it first hears from him and knows what he is doing, does it?" Using discretion, Nicodemus enlightened the Pharisees, who, based on their distorted views, were relentlessly arguing for their own positions. Although he was a Pharisee, Nicodemus was different. He tried to obey God's laws with a good heart.

The rest of the Pharisees, who thought Nicodemus was on their side, were shocked by what Nicodemus said, and for a moment they were taken aback. They tried to look for a strong refute, but because Nicodemus' argument was so sharp and to the point, they could not come up with any rebuttal. All they could say in reply was, "You are not also from Galilee, are you? Search, and see that no prophet arises out of Galilee." This was a weak answer belittling Jesus by calling Him a Galilean.

It's hard to believe that they did not know that Jesus was not born in Galilee. However, they could not make a logical and persuasive refutation against Nicodemus' argument, so that was all they could say. And with that, they dropped their dispute about Jesus, and they all returned to their homes. The conspiracy of those who wanted to capture Jesus, failed. In front of a good person of truth, any untruth—lies, deceit, and the like—all come out into the open. Wisdom from goodness is of God; therefore darkness can do nothing but flee from it.

Chapter 8

The Truth Will Make You Free

Jesus Forgives the Woman Who Committed Adultery

One day, Peter asked Jesus, *"Lord, how often shall my brother sin against me and I forgive him? Up to seven times?"* (Matthew 18:21). Peter thought that forgiving someone seven times was showing great compassion. But Jesus' answer went beyond Peter's imagination. He said, *"I do not say to you, up to seven times, but up to seventy times seven"* (v. 22).

Here, Jesus is not saying we should forgive someone 490 times. Seven is a perfect, or complete number. So forgiving seventy times seven signifies complete forgiveness, or forgiving an unlimited number of times. In the same way, Jesus not only did good deeds and gave life to people; but He also forgave sinners of their sins, and thereby helped those forgiven to feel the deep love of God.

The Sadducees and Pharisees Who Caught the Adulteress

> "But Jesus went to the Mount of Olives. Early in the morning He came again into the temple, and all the people were coming to Him; and He sat down and began to teach them. The scribes and the Pharisees brought a woman caught in adultery, and having set her in the center of the court, they said to Him, 'Teacher, this woman has been caught in adultery, in the very act. Now in the Law Moses commanded us to stone such women; what then do You say?'" (John 8:1-5)

After His message at the Feast of Tabernacles, Jesus went to the Mount of Olives. The Mount of Olives, which is located in the eastern part of Jerusalem, got its name because of the unusually large number of olive trees there. At the peak of the mountain, one can see the entire city of Jerusalem with a single glance. This is where Jesus gave His sermons about the gospel of Heaven, and this is also where He cried as He prophesied about the events to come. It is a significant place as it seems Jesus' footprints are embedded there.

The Mount of Olives is also a valuable place in the history of Israel. Zechariah 14:1-5 mentions that the Messiah will stand on it, and the Prophet Ezekiel also said that he saw in a vision that the glory of the LORD will be there. At the foot of the Mount of Olives is Gethsemane, where Jesus often went to pray. This is where Jesus prayed so fervently that His sweat became

: : Mount of Olives, located in the eastern part of Jerusalem

like drops of blood, the night before He was captured to be crucified.

After praying at the Mount of Olives in the night, Jesus returned to the temple in the morning. While He was teaching the people there, a great commotion occurred. The Sadducees and Pharisees fought through the crowd and brought a woman to Jesus. Pushing her into the center of attention, they said haphazardly, "Teacher, this woman has been caught in adultery, in the very act."

According to the Law of Moses, whether male or female, a person committing adultery was put to death (Leviticus 20:10). The Sadducees and Pharisees asked to apply this law to the woman. The woman shook for shame and fear of death, as her sins were publicly displayed for all to see. However, the Sadducees and Pharisees did not care about her life. They were feeling quite triumphant because, by using the Law they now had a pretext to test Jesus.

He Who is Without Sin, Let Him Be the First to Throw a Stone

"They were saying this, testing Him, so that they might have grounds for accusing Him. But Jesus stooped down and with His finger wrote on the ground. But when they persisted in asking Him, He straightened up, and said to them, 'He who is without sin among you, let him be the first to throw a stone at her.' Again He stooped down and wrote on the ground." (8:6-8)

In actuality, the Sadducees and Pharisees were at a crisis stage since so many people were beginning to follow Jesus. In comparison to their teachings, Jesus' teachings were incomparably more powerful. On top of that, Jesus was reprimanding them, so as leaders of the people, they were in an uncomfortable situation. So as their antagonistic feelings against Jesus began piling up, they began searching every corner for a way to catch Jesus off-guard. After capturing a woman committing adultery, they seized this event as a great opportunity to test Jesus.

Instead of focusing on the sin of the woman who committed

adultery, they were focused on trying to find some kind of fault in Jesus' reaction. They thought they knew to some degree what His reaction would be like. They knew that according to His usual teachings, He would tell them not to stone her. If at this time, Jesus had said, "Love, forgive," what would happen? Then He would sound like He was speaking against the Law of Moses, which would give them a good reason to accuse Him. Going against the Law was considered the grave sin of being hostile toward God's Word. So this was a golden opportunity to find grounds for accusation against Jesus based on the Law.

If Jesus went against their expectations and said, "Stone her," according to the Law, this would also give them reason to accuse Him, because it would be going against His usual teachings about love and forgiveness. The Sadducees and Pharisees asked Jesus what to do, knowing full well that the situation would cause some sort of dilemma, where Jesus wouldn't be able to say this or that. And so they thought they had Jesus in their trap.

To these people who were insisting on an answer, Jesus didn't say a word. Instead, He stooped down and began writing something on the ground with His finger. For a moment, there was silence. After a while, He stood up, and looking around at the crowd, He said, "He who is without sin among you, let him be the first to throw a stone at her." Then He stooped down, and wrote on the ground with His finger once more. And then what do you think happened?

The People Who Received the Pangs of Conscience

"When they heard it, they began to go out one by one, beginning with the older ones, and He was left alone, and the woman, where she was, in the center of the court." (8:9)

The people who had gathered there began to depart one by one. The Sadducees and Pharisees who were feeling triumphant just moments before, and the people who were just curious about what was going on, all left quietly, as if they felt a bit ashamed. Just what did Jesus write on the ground that caused everyone to feel such pangs of conscience? What He had written pointed out their sins.

Jesus knew even the smallest sin that people committed. As if He could see the sins that everyone there had in common, He began writing them down, one by one. The reason why He wrote the sins on the ground as opposed to saying them out loud, was because it was God's will not to include them in the Bible.

While God commands us not to weigh, judge, or condemn others, if Jesus had pointed out each person's sins in minute detail, and all of it had been recorded in the Bible, what could have happened? Could the people not have used such a response as evidence against Jesus and accused Him of judgment and condemnation? That is why Jesus did not call out and uncover each of their sins, but He rather wrote them down on the ground, so no evidence would be left behind.

The people who were pointing out the woman's wrongdoing and calling out for the penalty of her sin suddenly realized that they themselves were sinners who should be stoned as well. Feeling ashamed, the people quietly slipped away. Finally, everyone left, leaving only Jesus and the woman.

Jesus Gives the Woman a Chance to Repent

"Straightening up, Jesus said to her, 'Woman, where are they? Did no one condemn you?' She said, 'No one, Lord.' And Jesus said, 'I do not condemn you either. Go. From now on sin no more.'" (8:10-11)

When the people who were condemning and accusing the adulteress felt ashamed and had departed, leaving her all alone, Jesus spoke and befittingly told her, "I do not condemn you either. Go and from now on, sin no more." To the woman shaking from shame and fear, Jesus' words were probably like a single ray of sunlight. When Jesus says here that He does not condemn her, it means that He forgives her. Then why did Jesus forgive her and not condemn her according to the Law? It is because God is a God of justice and love.

According to the Law, the woman had to die to pay for the penalty of her sin, but by forgiving her, Jesus was giving her a chance to repent and turn from her ways. God's purpose for sending His only begotten Son, Jesus, into this world was not to condemn the sinners and put them to death, but to give them a chance to repent and receive eternal life (John 3:17, 12:47).

So while forgiving the woman for her sins, at the same time, Jesus stressed the importance of true repentance, where one leaves a life of evil for good. If we get into the habit of continuing to sin while knowing it is a sin and then repent afterwards, only to repeat the action again, then that is not true repentance. No matter what kind of sin we might have committed, it is very important to turn away from that sin and live according to God's Word as soon as possible.

Jesus' Message for the Jews

The High Priests and the Pharisees wondered how they could find fault with Jesus; so they often threw questions at Him that just might make Him slip and fall into their trap. Asking what to do with the woman caught committing adultery, and whether it is right or wrong to pay taxes to Caesar, are some good examples of this. They even plotted together to see how they might trap Jesus (Matthew 22:15).

But each time, Jesus not only gave unexpected and very wise replies and avoided their traps, but He always enlightened them with the truth. No matter what situation He was in, as the Son of God, who is Light, Jesus fulfilled the Law with love, and only acted in accordance with God's will.

I Am the Light of the World

"Then Jesus again spoke to them, saying, 'I am the Light of the world; he who follows Me will not walk in the darkness, but will have the Light of life.' So the Pharisees said to Him, 'You are testifying about Yourself; Your testimony is not true.'" (8:12-13)

Light has the power to chase away the dark. When there is light, there is no room for darkness. Light controls, conquers, and rules over darkness. In 1 John 1:5 is recorded, *"God is Light."* Therefore, Jesus, who is one with God, is also Light. And the reason why Jesus called Himself the "Light of the world" was because the world is in the midst of darkness. Only Jesus has the power to cast out darkness, and He Himself is the Light. So, why is the world in the midst of darkness? In 1 John 2:15-16 it says, *"Do not love the world nor the things in the world. If anyone loves the world, the love of the Father is not in him. For all that is in the world, the lust of the flesh and the lust of the eyes and the boastful pride of life, is not from the Father, but is from the world."*

"Lust of the flesh" signifies the sinful nature that goes contrary to God's will and causes man to sin. For example, laziness, adultery, debauchery, hate, jealousy, envy, greed, gossiping, etc., are all desires of the heart that cause man to want to sin. If the lust of the flesh is not gotten rid of, one day it may be agitated and cause the person to commit sin in actions. For example, if someone has greed, and he sees an object that he really wants, he may go out of his way to get it, even if it means going into debt, or stealing.

"Lust of the eyes" is an attribute of one of the sinful natures that causes man to want something after the heart is incited by seeing something with the eyes, or hearing something with the ears. We occasionally hear news about someone who commits a crime after watching a violent movie. After seeing the movie, the desire to imitate the action in the movie, or the "lust of the eyes" was agitated in him, provoking commission of the crime.

"The boastful pride of life" is the sinful nature that causes man to want to boast about himself, while seeking all the pleasures of this world. Most of the time, people want to show off their family name, education, or abilities. But these kinds of desires are from the ruler of the dark world, the enemy devil. Therefore people who follow the lust of the flesh and seek the pleasures of this world will one day receive God's judgment and meet everlasting death.

On the other hand, light is the opposite of darkness. It is life and truth, and it represents God's Word. Just as light brightens up the darkness, although we were once living in the midst of untruth, when God's Word enlightens us about sin, righteousness, and judgment, we can walk toward the way of truth, life, and righteousness. That is why Jesus said, "He who follows Me will not walk in the darkness, but will have the Light of life." What He means by this is that people who leave the darkness and live in the Light, according to God's Word, according to Jesus' teachings, can receive eternal life.

Light also signifies the aroma of Christ. As much as one leaves the dark and lives more in the Light, that's how much more they can lead other people to the Light and truth (Matthew 5:14-15). Just like butterflies smell the aroma of flowers and gather around flowers, people who love and seek the truth will gather around the Light.

When Jesus said He was the Light of the world, the Pharisees condemned Him, saying His testimony was not valid, because He was testifying about Himself. At that time, in Israel, a witness's testimony played a very important role during legal proceedings. If a witness was ever caught giving a false testimony, that witness had to receive the punishment in place of the defendant. That's how much truth and responsibility was required of a witness. The witness had to have an objective stance between the defendant and the accuser, so in most cases, the court only recognized witnesses from a third party. This was done to draw out only fair and credible testimonies devoid of any bias.

This is the very reason the Pharisees condemned Jesus' testimony. However, in the beginning of Jesus' public ministry, there weren't many people who knew Jesus. Of course John the Baptist prepared the way for the Lord, but not long after, John was decapitated by King Herod. Also, this was before the coming of the Holy Spirit, so there was no one led by the Spirit to spread the word about Jesus. That is why Jesus showed that He was the Son of God as He spread the gospel of Heaven.

I am Not Judging Anyone

> "Jesus answered and said to them, 'Even if I testify about Myself, My testimony is true, for I know where I came from and where I am going; but you do not know where I come from or where I am going. You judge according to the flesh; I am not judging anyone. But even if I do judge, My judgment is true; for I am not alone in it, but I and the Father who sent Me.'" (8:14-16)

Most people rarely do what they say they're going to do. So, when someone says, "I am this kind of person," other people don't believe him, because they assume that this person is just like themselves. So in order to test the validity of another person, people look at his or her achievements or the vestiges of his past actions.

But Jesus always told the truth. He never added or took away from what He actually saw. He told people that He came from God, and He showed them the way to salvation. He not only used His words, but He also performed signs and wonders that are humanly impossible to perform, and proved the validity of His words. Wherever He went, evidences of His truthfulness showed. When He forgave sinners, their illnesses or infirmities were cured, and the lives of everyone who met Him changed forever. Also, Jesus knew where He came from and where He was going. He knew the beginning and the end, the origin, and the process and conclusion of everything.

What about the Pharisees? They did not know where

Jesus had come from or why He came. On top of that, they tried to understand His spiritual messages with their worldly logic and knowledge, so they simply could not understand. So they themselves became the judge and began judging and condemning Jesus.

Jesus told them exactly what their problem was. He told them that they were judging based on the flesh. Judging based on the flesh means judging someone's character or value based on outward appearances or conditions. It is coming to a conclusion about someone's character based on their physical appearance, possessions, position or what other people say about them.

That is why after simply seeing the outward actions of the woman caught committing adultery, the Pharisees came to the conclusion that according to the Law she had to be stoned. They were never concerned about what kinds of difficulties the woman might have had, or what surrounding circumstances or situations she might have been in. They considered the laws more valuable than people, and judging more correct and valuable than forgiveness and love. Likewise, people of the flesh see everything based on their logic and thoughts, therefore they end up making wrong judgments and committing evil.

On the contrary, all of Jesus' judgments were true. He is the Word that became flesh. He is the truth itself. Therefore He could be, do or speak nothing other than the truth. Jesus' judgment was true because just as He said, "For I am not alone in it, but I and the Father who sent Me," God was with Him. Jesus said this because although He had the power to judge, the ultimate judge over everything is God and God only.

Jesus came to this world not to be its judge, but to take up all the sins of mankind unto Himself and receive the penalty of death on the behalf of all mankind. Because He had to take up the cross to receive all the curses that the sinners were supposed to receive, He did not say, "I am originally one with God, therefore my judgment is true." If He had said, "I am God, so my judgment is correct," what would have happened? Jesus knew how the Jews would react; therefore, in order to prevent them from misunderstanding or falling into temptation, He spoke with wisdom.

If You Knew Me, You Would Know My Father Also

"'Even in your law it has been written that the testimony of two men is true. I am He who testifies about Myself, and the Father who sent Me testifies about Me.' So they were saying to Him, 'Where is Your Father?' Jesus answered, 'You know neither Me nor My Father; if you knew Me, you would know My Father also.' These words He spoke in the treasury, as He taught in the temple; and no one seized Him, because His hour had not yet come." (8:17-20)

In order to conduct a fair trial according to the Law, two or more witnesses are necessary (Deuteronomy 17:6, 19:15). That is why with signs and wonders, Jesus Himself testified that He was the Son of God; and since God was His other witness, He stated that according to the Law, His testimony was valid.

How did God act as Jesus' witness? If you look at Matthew chapter 3, there is a scene where Jesus was coming out of the water after being baptized. At that time, a voice out of the heavens said, *"This is My beloved Son, in whom I am well-pleased"* (v. 17). And during Jesus' public ministry, God manifested many wonders that only He could do, in order to prove that Jesus is His Son, and that everything He said was true.

But not understanding Jesus' words, the Pharisees asked, "Where is your father?" When Jesus talked about "the Father who sent Me," the Pharisees thought Jesus was talking about His physical father. They didn't know the spiritual meaning behind Jesus' words, and they couldn't understand why Jesus was calling God His 'Father.'

At this point, the chief priests and Pharisees were trying to arrest Jesus at even the smallest opportunity given to them. But, even though Jesus taught the people and appeared in public places like the temple, still no one dared to arrest Him. This was because it was not yet time for Him to take the suffering on the cross. Because all things are under God's authority, until God permitted it, no one could apprehend Jesus.

The Prophecy about Jesus' Death on the Cross, His Resurrection, and Ascension

"Then He said again to them, 'I go away, and you will seek Me, and will die in your sin; where I am going, you cannot come.' So the Jews were saying, 'Surely He

will not kill Himself, will He, since He says, "Where I am going, you cannot come"?'" (8:21-22)

After testifying that He was the Son of God, Jesus then said something with a little more spiritual depth. He told them about His death on the cross, His resurrection, and His ascension. "I go away, and you will seek Me, and will die in your sin."

The "you" here is referring to the Jews who were against Him. They earnestly sought for the Messiah, but though the Messiah stood right in front of them, they didn't even recognize Him! They rather ridiculed Him, though He was the Messiah, thinking that He was a son of a poor carpenter and a friend of the weak and for the sinners.

That is why as Jesus said, "I go away, and you will seek Me, and will die in your sin," He felt very sad for them [Jews], because they were going the way of death. When Jesus said that they will die because of their sin, He was letting them know that they were not only spiritually very ignorant; but their hearts were full of envy and evil, and because they denied the Christ, they would die in the midst of pain and despair.

Jesus also said, "Where I am going, you cannot come," telling them about His ascension after dying on the cross. However, the Jews did not understand this, and they thought Jesus was about to take His own life. To them, the fact that Jesus, who only looked like the son of a poor carpenter, would be ascending into heaven, was beyond their imagination. In this same way a person of the flesh will come up with one random speculation after another.

I Am Who I've Been Telling You That I Was From the Beginning

> "And He was saying to them, 'You are from below, I am from above; you are of this world, I am not of this world. Therefore I said to you that you will die in your sins; for unless you believe that I am He, you will die in your sins.' So they were saying to Him, 'Who are You?' Jesus said to them, 'What have I been saying to you from the beginning?'" (8:23-25)

When Jesus used the word "below" here, He was referring to the ground, and "You are from below", means that they [Jews] were born into this world from parents of the flesh; and they learned the things of the flesh, which they stored up as knowledge. This is why they could not understand, nor believe the things that Jesus said regarding the fourth dimension, or the spiritual world. Unlike them, Jesus was born from above. Since He was conceived by the Holy Spirit through God's power, from the time of His birth all was done in the Spirit. In John 7:15, the Jews asked, *"How has this man become learned, having never been educated?"* Instead of the teachings of man, Jesus only acted in the truth and God's Word, which shows that He is not of this world.

When Jesus said, "Unless you believe that I am He, you will die in your sins," the Jews asked, "Who are You?" To this, Jesus asked in return, "What have I been saying to you from the beginning?" Jesus tried to remind them about what He had been telling them all along—that He is the Messiah whom the

Old Testament prophesied about, the One whom the Jews had been waiting for all this time.

So now, let's take a look at how the Old Testament prophesied about the Messiah, and examine how the New Testament has been the fulfillment of what was prophesied about Him.

If you look at Genesis 3:15, it says, *"And I will put enmity between you and the woman, and between your seed and her seed; He shall bruise you on the head, and you shall bruise him on the heel."* This is what God said to the serpent, who tempted Eve to eat the fruit of the knowledge of good and evil. Here, the serpent represents the enemy devil and Satan, and the woman represents Israel. This is a prophecy that says the Messiah will be born into Israel and have victory over the enemy devil. This is exactly what happened (Galatians 4:4-5). Jesus Christ, from the lineage of a woman, was born into the nation of Israel. He shattered the power of death, which was under the authority of the enemy devil and Satan, and resurrected from the dead, and thus He ultimately completed God's plan of salvation.

Also, as it is written in Isaiah 7:14, *"Therefore the Lord Himself will give you a sign: Behold, a virgin will be with child and bear a son,"* Jesus was born of the Virgin Mary. On top of that, as recorded in Jeremiah 31:15, King Herod shed the blood of countless children at the time of Jesus' birth (Matthew 2:16).

The fact that Jesus would perform many signs to show God's power is recorded in Isaiah 35:5-6, and even the fact that Judas

Iscariot would sell Jesus for thirty silver coins is prophesied in Zechariah 11:12. And, Jesus' resurrection and ascension are prophesied in other areas of the Bible as well (Psalms 16:10, 68:18).

Therefore, history confirms that all the prophecies about Jesus occurred exactly as they had said they would. Just reading a few verses in the Bible lets us know and believe that Jesus is the Savior who came to save mankind. As the Messiah, Jesus even knew what was in the deepest part of the Jews' hearts. That's why He was able to judge them with the truth. However, He did not condemn them with ill emotions. Instead, He tried all He could to lead them to the truth.

He Who Sent Me is With Me

"'I have many things to speak and to judge concerning you, but He who sent Me is true; and the things which I heard from Him, these I speak to the world.' They did not realize that He had been speaking to them about the Father. So Jesus said, 'When you lift up the Son of Man, then you will know that I am He, and I do nothing on My own initiative, but I speak these things as the Father taught Me. And He who sent Me is with Me; He has not left Me alone, for I always do the things that are pleasing to Him.' As He spoke these things, many came to believe in Him." (8:26-30)

"He who sent Me," refers to God, and "the things which I heard from Him," refers to the truth. However, the Jews did not realize that the person Jesus was talking about was the Father God. In order to share the truth as much as He could, and to save at least one more soul, there were times when Jesus preached the gospel of Heaven without even eating or sleeping. He always did what pleased God; and that is why God never left His side.

What pleased God about Jesus was that He lowered Himself and completely submitted to God's will in everything He did. This is also the reason why so many people believed and followed Jesus, with the exception of the Pharisees and Sadducees who had evil hearts.

The Freedom in the Truth

Truth, according to the world, has been changing, and changing according to the changing of time and circumstances. At one time, people thought that Geocentric Theory was the truth. But with the advancement of science, the Heliocentric Theory became the new truth. But there is a truth that is unchanging. And that truth is the Word of God. Knowing this truth not only means learning and knowing God's Word; but it also means understanding God's will, casting out evil, and acting in the truth.

Truth's Freedom: Knowing the Truth Will Give You Freedom

"So Jesus was saying to those Jews who had believed Him, 'If you continue in My word, then you are truly disciples of Mine; and you will know the truth, and the truth will make you free.'" (8:31-32)

The Jews thought that as long as they obeyed the Law, they would be acknowledged as God's people, and that they would receive salvation. But they did not cast away evils from the heart. So Jesus said to them, "If you continue in My word, then you are truly disciples of Mine," letting them know what true salvation is. Salvation is only possible when one believes in Jesus Christ. When we believe in Jesus Christ, we are forgiven of our sins, and when we act according to the truth, we become true disciples of the Lord, and we can go to Heaven.

"Continue in My word," means to love, pray, cast out envy, jealousy, hate, etc., according to the Word; and it means to abide by the commandments. Only when we abide in Jesus, seeking the truth and acting in the light, can we become a true disciple of Jesus and say we truly "know the truth". Putting up God's Word on their doorposts and gates, and tying His Word to their wrists to meditate and obey them day and night, the Jews boasted of knowing the truth. But, they obeyed the Law without really understanding God's will.

Physically obeying God's laws without really understanding God's good and perfect will contained within those laws is like throwing away the grain and eating the husk. For example, because the Jews did not know God's will for giving man the Sabbath day, they condemned Jesus for performing a good deed on the Sabbath day. They did not obey the laws out of joy. They obeyed the laws out of a sense of duty, or for fear of being punished if they don't obey the laws. Their lifestyles were just tied down by the old customs and traditions that were handed down to them from their ancestors. How sad Jesus must have been, knowing all of this! That is why He said to them, "You will know the truth, and the truth will make you free."

In the course of daily life, no one remembers every single criterion under every single law and checks to see if he is in compliance with the law every time he takes a step. People usually just live naturally obeying the law. That is as long as the law does not confine us and we live with freedom. This is the same for our spiritual lives. When there is untruth in our hearts, that's how much freedom we don't have, and we continue to live as a slave to sin. As much as we have evil in our hearts, that's how much we're going against God's Word, so we need to constantly scrutinize what's inside of ourselves. How difficult would it be to have to question whether something is a sin or not, before making each and every move? However, if we cast out the untruth from our hearts and fill it with truth, then even if we don't question and reason every law and detail, we are not condemned.

Just as someone who excels at abiding by the laws is never restrained by the laws, when we abide by God's Word, the truth sets us free. If we don't have hate, envy, jealousy, or discord, and we don't stumble in any circumstances and we can be at peace with everyone, then there is true peace in our lives, and we can be joyful. This is what it means to gain freedom by knowing the truth.

Everyone Who Sins Is a Slave of Sin

"They answered Him, 'We are Abraham's descendants and have never yet been enslaved to anyone; how is it that You say, "You will become free"? Jesus answered them, 'Truly, truly, I say to you, everyone who commits sin is the slave of sin. The slave does not remain in the house forever; the son does remain forever. So if the Son makes you free, you will be free indeed.'" (8:33-36)

Jesus was saying that the joy and happiness one has when living in the truth is "freedom", in a spiritual sense. But the Jews took this literally, and thought He was talking about becoming someone's slave and then being set free. That is why they were quick to say that as Abraham's descendants, they were never enslaved to anyone.

To this, Jesus answered, "Everyone who commits sin is the slave of sin," and He let them know that they are sinners. But why do we become slaves to sin? There is a spiritual order that says, *"you are slaves of the one whom you obey"* (Romans 6:16). If we obey the enemy devil and Satan, who is the overseer of sin, and commit a sin, then we become a slave of the devil and Satan, and a slave of sin.

Slaves must submit to their master. Even if they are bought and sold like animals, they cannot resist. And due to the enemy devil and Satan's accusations, slaves of sin experience many problems, and illnesses creep into their lives. Then, ultimately, because the wages of sin is death, they end up in Hell, where the fire never dies

On the other hand, the master's son enjoys all the good things with his father, and later receives his inheritance. When we become free from the slavery of sin and become a child of God, then we not only get to carry on a free life in the love of God the Father, who wants to give us all good things, but ultimately, we also receive Heaven as our inheritance.

Up until this point, Jesus did not directly reveal who He was. Jesus knew that if He told the people that He came to this world as God's Son, there would be someone who would either fall into temptation or accuse Him; and He found no reason to incite this type of interference. But in this part of the text, He plainly tells everyone that He is the one that gives freedom, and that He is God's Son. Why did He do this? He did this because among those who were listening to Him at that time, many had become believers.

In order to save all mankind from sin, Jesus died on the cross. And, defeating the power of death, He resurrected. Just as it is written in Romans 8:1-2, because Jesus freed us from the laws of sin and death, as long as we are in Christ Jesus, we no longer stand accused, but have true freedom.

If You Are Abraham's Children

"'I know that you are Abraham's descendants; yet you seek to kill Me, because My word has no place in you. I speak the things which I have seen with My Father; therefore you also do the things which you

heard from your father.' They answered and said to Him, 'Abraham is our father.' Jesus said to them, 'If you are Abraham's children, do the deeds of Abraham. But as it is, you are seeking to kill Me, a man who has told you the truth, which I heard from God; this Abraham did not do.'" (8:37-40)

At that time, the Jews were very proud of being the descendants of Abraham. They also were not very fond of Jesus. If at this time Jesus had said, "You don't have the qualification of being Abraham's descendants," they would have become even more disgruntled. That is why Jesus first acknowledged their stance, saying, "I know that you are Abraham's descendants," and then He continued to teach them. By saying, "Yet you seek to kill Me, because My word has no place in you," Jesus tried to help them turn from their wrong ways on their own.

Instead of being direct, Jesus used an indirect approach to point out their wrongs; and while doing so, He let them know that all of His words came from God (John 5:19-20, 12:49). Then He told them that they were doing things that came from the enemy devil and Satan. However, they replied, "Abraham is our father."

The Jews acted holy and clean on the outside, in order to look upright before men, but deep inside their hearts, they were filled with ostentation, lawlessness, greed, and debauchery. But Abraham showed complete submission to God's Word, and he followed God's every lead—to the point of being called a friend of God. He was giving to the point of giving his nephew, Lot, the better land, by allowing him to pick first. And when Sodom and Gomorrah were on the verge of destruction, He asked God for mercy; interceding for the people living there. He was a true man of faith, who was even willing to sacrifice his son Isaac, whom he begot at the age of one hundred, when God asked for him.

If the Jews were so proud of having such an ancestor, they should have tried to follow his actions. They called Abraham their 'father', and yet they were trying to kill Jesus, who was telling them the truth which He heard from the Father God. Jesus was trying to show the Jews this very contradictory image of themselves.

If God Were Your Father

"'You are doing the deeds of your father.' They said to Him, 'We were not born of fornication; we have one Father: God.' Jesus said to them, 'If God were your Father, you would love Me, for I proceeded forth and have come from God, for I have not even come on My own initiative, but He sent Me.'" (8:41-42)

Here, the word 'father' literally means a parent, but spiritually, it means the devil. The master of the fallen man is the enemy devil. 1 John 3:8 says, *"The one who practices sin is of the devil; for the devil has sinned from the beginning. The Son of God appeared for this purpose: to destroy the works of the devil."* The 'works of the devil' refers to all the different sizes and shapes of evil that come about as a result of sin. People of God rejoice when they see something that is upright, and they joyfully follow what is right. However, the Jews were trying to kill Jesus, and that is why Jesus said they were doing works of the devil.

The Jews defended themselves, saying, "We were not born of fornication; we have one Father: God." What the Jews mean by "fornication" is bowing down to other gods and worshipping false idols. When we look at the Old Testament, whenever there is a warning against worshipping false idols, words such as "fornication" or "prostitution" is used (Judges 2:17; Ezekiel 23:30). Because the Jews were confident that they were living in strict adherence to the laws, unlike these ancestors who opposed God, they boldly called God their "Father".

Then Jesus taught them what they needed to do in order to be able to truly call God their "Father". Jesus said, "If God were your Father, you would love Me." Why do you think Jesus said this? It's because God sent Jesus. People who truly love God do not obey the laws out of formality, but they obey with a true desire to obey God from the center of their hearts. Because they have goodness in their hearts, people like these recognized Jesus who came as the Christ (Luke 2:25-38). The Jews obeyed the laws, but because they did it out of formality, and they did not cast out any evil from their hearts, even though Jesus was right in front of their eyes, they did not recognize Him.

Why Do You Not Understand?

"Why do you not understand what I am saying? It is because you cannot hear My word. You are of your father the devil, and you want to do the desires of your father. He was a murderer from the beginning, and does not stand in the truth because there is no truth in him. Whenever he speaks a lie, he speaks from his own nature, for he is a liar and the father of lies." (8:43-44)

The Jews were so set on their theories and opinions that they didn't even try to listen to Jesus' words. Even though they confirmed God's power working through Jesus, they did not acknowledge it, and even though Jesus told them He was the Christ, they didn't believe Him. If it didn't benefit them, they didn't want to accept it, even though it was right. If they had a selfish desire for something that was beneficial to them, they did whatever they could to obtain it, disregarding what happened to other people. Jesus taught them that this was due to the selfish desires that came from the devil.

The words "murderer from the beginning" and "liar" clearly pinpoint the enemy devil and Satan's characteristics. The enemy devil and Satan enticed the serpent to use crafty lies to seduce Eve to disobey God's Word. Satan breathed out the lust of the flesh, lust of the eyes, and pride of this life into man. Satan also ignited Cain's jealousy, which eventually caused him to kill his younger brother. From then on, Satan just continued to tempt people to become tainted with sin. The Jews thought for themselves that they had strong faith in God, and they regarded

Jesus as a liar claiming to be God's son. That is why Jesus used the words of truth to expose their inner heart. He helped them to see the fact that because they were filled with lies and selfish desires that provoked them to seek after things that benefit only themselves, they were of the devil.

Which One of You Convicts Me of Sin?

> **"But because I speak the truth, you do not believe Me. Which one of you convicts Me of sin? If I speak truth, why do you not believe Me? He who is of God hears the words of God; for this reason you do not hear them, because you are not of God." (8:45-47)**

A person of truth recognizes another person's sincerity and believes that person. The reason the Jews didn't believe Jesus even though He spoke the truth, was because they themselves were not truthful. Whenever they had the chance, in an attempt to convict Jesus, the high priest, the priests, and the Pharisees tested Him by throwing cunning questions at Him. But each time, they fell into a frustrating situation where they could not come up with a good reply to Jesus' words of truth. To this, Jesus asks, "If I speak truth, why do you not believe Me?"

A person of God believes in God's Word and acts in goodness. 1 John 4:7 says, *"For love is from God."* Aside from love, the characteristics of goodness, justice, truth, faith, etc., are all from God as well. God is always in the light. He is also good and righteous. When people of God come before Him, they change. But love, goodness, and righteousness, could not be found in the Jews. The fact that they did not believe in Jesus, who was speaking the truth, proves that they were not of God.

The Jews Try to Stone Jesus

One form of public execution that the Jews used at the time was stoning. According to the Law, there were seventeen crimes for which stoning was applied as a form of punishment; some of which were desecration, idol worship, breaking the Sabbath, sorcery, adultery, etc. Not understanding Jesus' Words, they thought He was guilty of desecration. So they thought they could stone at Jesus according to the Law.

I Do Not Have a Demon

"The Jews answered and said to Him, 'Do we not say rightly that You are a Samaritan and have a demon?' Jesus answered, 'I do not have a demon; but I honor

My Father, and you dishonor Me. But I do not seek My glory; there is One who seeks and judges.'" (8:48-50)

When Jesus plainly exposed the Jews' spiritual state out into the open, they began twisting with anger inside. This is why they retorted with evil words against Jesus. "Do we not say rightly that You are a Samaritan and have a demon?"

During those days, in the Jewish society, calling someone a "Samaritan" was highly derogatory. Typically, when people argue with one another and their emotions get heated up, they call each other names of things that they normally think are bad or negative from their everyday life. Some people say, "You're a dog!" or "You're a scoundrel!" Now when the Jews called Jesus a "Samaritan", this was the same case.

On top of that, they accused Jesus of "having a demon". This shows that the evil in their hearts had reached its max. But even to their evil comments, Jesus only said, "I do not have a demon; but I honor My Father, and you dishonor Me." He was teaching them that with everything He did, He did it with a heart that honors the Father, not a heart seeking after His own glory.

As needed, there were times when Jesus showed that He was God's Son, and there were times when He forgave sins. Seeing this, the Jews mistook Him as someone who sought to receive His own glory. That is why He said, "But I do not seek My glory." And when He said, "There is One who seeks and judges," it means that when Jesus seeks God's glory, God also glorifies Jesus.

Whom Do You Make Yourself Out To Be?

"'Truly, truly, I say to you, if anyone keeps My word he will never see death.' The Jews said to Him, 'Now we know that You have a demon. Abraham died, and the prophets also; and You say, "If anyone keeps My word, he will never taste of death." Surely You are not greater than our father Abraham, who died? The prophets died too; whom do You make Yourself out to be?'" (8:51-53)

Keeping Jesus' Word affects whether our spirits live or die. If we believe in Jesus, who is the resurrection and the life, and we live by His Word, we receive eternal life and live eternally in Heaven (John 11:25-26). That is why Jesus said, "If anyone keeps My word, he will never taste of death."

The Jews had no idea what this meant. And once again, they compared Jesus to Abraham, and then accused Him of having a demon. They said, "You say, 'If anyone keeps My word, he will never taste of death.' Surely You are not greater than our father Abraham, who died?' The prophets died too; whom do You make Yourself out to be?" Yes, these Jews were descendants of Abraham, but God did not acknowledge them. God does not acknowledge someone based on their bloodline or their mere act of obeying the laws. He acknowledges those people who actually live in righteousness with true faith (Romans 4:13, 16).

It Is My Father Who Glorifies Me

> "Jesus answered, 'If I glorify Myself, My glory is nothing; it is My Father who glorifies Me, of whom you say, "He is our God"; and you have not come to know Him, but I know Him; and if I say that I do not know Him, I will be a liar like you, but I do know Him and keep His word.'" (8:54-55)

Those who boast about themselves or show themselves off have hard time earning the trust of those around them. People often think they are either exaggerating, or lying altogether. That is why Jesus also said, "If I glorify Myself, My glory is nothing," and He revealed that God is the One who glorifies Him. But when He said this, He didn't just call God "God", but "My Father", "Of whom you say, 'He is our God'".

At this time, the Jews were infuriated with Jesus, and they considered Him as someone who had nothing to do with God; and they were insisting that He was demon-possessed. They sensed the crisis and were ready to threaten Him directly.

If in this situation Jesus had felt frightened, stepped back, and said, "I don't know God," then He would become a liar, just like them. But there is no way that Jesus—who is God Himself—didn't know God. And as a final confirmation that His Word was true, He said, "I do know Him and keep His word." Now Jesus was explaining what He wanted to say in a very clear and "to-the-point" kind of way.

The Jews Try to Stone Jesus

> "'Your father Abraham rejoiced to see My day, and he saw it and was glad.' So the Jews said to Him, 'You are not yet fifty years old, and have You seen Abraham?' Jesus said to them, 'Truly, truly, I say to you, before Abraham was born, I am.' Therefore they picked up stones to throw at Him, but Jesus hid Himself and went out of the temple." (8:56-59)

Since the Jews were talking about Abraham, Jesus tried to relate with them by talking about Abraham as well. In Genesis 22:18, God made a covenant with Abraham, saying, *"In your seed all the nations of the earth shall be blessed."* But the heir of Abraham is not by bloodline or through the Law, but through the righteousness of faith (Romans 4:13). So in order to fulfill this, Jesus had to complete the plan of salvation.

Abraham, who used to have deep conversations with God, knew that the covenant He received from Him would be fulfilled a long time after his own lifetime, through Jesus Christ. So of course he was rejoicing and longing for the coming of Jesus! However, to the Jews, who had no knowledge of the spiritual world, this was unbelievable! So they asked how a person who is not yet fifty has seen Abraham, who lived 2,000 years ago.

To this, Jesus answered, "Truly, truly, I say to you, before Abraham was born, I am." This is true. Although Jesus was born in the flesh two thousand years after Abraham, in the spirit, He existed way before. This is because Jesus was with God from the very beginning of time. So Jesus was just telling them the truth as it was, but the Jews could not hold their anger any longer, and they picked up stones to throw at Jesus. They became irate and tried to kill Him because they misunderstood His spiritual Words. But because it was not His time yet, Jesus left the temple to avoid these men full of malice.

Chapter 9

Jesus Heals a Blind Man

Go, Wash in the Pool of Siloam

In the Bible, there are people whose lives changed 180 degrees after meeting Jesus. In addition to the twelve disciples, there was the woman who had suffered from a hemorrhage for twelve years and there was the blind beggar, Bartimaeus. Another one of these people who was changed was a man who had been blind from birth.

The Cause of Illness

"As he went along, he saw a man blind from birth. His disciples asked him, 'Rabbi, who sinned, this man or his parents, that he was born blind?'" (John 9:1-2)

One day, as Jesus was walking, He met a blind man. He's been blind since birth. Because he came from a poor family, he lived day to day as a beggar. Seeing him, the disciples became curious, and asked Jesus, "Rabbi, who sinned, this man or his parents?" Each time Jesus healed the sick, the crippled, or the demon-possessed He mentioned something about sin. When He healed the man at the pool of Bethsaida who was crippled for 38 years, He told him not to sin anymore. When He healed the paralytic, He said, *"Your sins are forgiven"* (Mark 2:5). We know from Mark chapter 2 that Jesus first solved the problem of sin. So through these events, the disciples came to learn that diseases, infirmities, and disabilities came as a result of sin.

'Disease' according to the Bible, is an abnormality in the body that makes the body sick, usually caused by poison, or some sort of virus. 'Infirmity' and 'disability' are when the body is unable to carry out normal activities because an organ in the body is either paralyzed or disabled due to a mistake made by the person, or the person's parent, or an accident. These types of disabilities are categorized as being either innate disabilities or acquired disabilities. In Deuteronomy chapter 28 lays out several types of curses that can come upon a person if he does not obey God's Word and does not follow His commands and decrees. This is because when a person sins, the enemy devil and Satan bring accusations against him as a result of his sin.

The following verses give an overall definition of sin according to the Bible: *"whatever is not from faith is sin"* (Romans 14:23); *"to one who knows the right thing to do and does not do it, to him it is sin"* (James 4:17); and *"For the good that I want, I do not do, but I practice the very evil that I do not want. But if I am doing the very thing I do not want, I am no longer the one doing it, but sin which dwells in me "* (Romans 7:19-20). And sin includes "deeds of the flesh" (Galatians 5:19-21) and "the things of the flesh" (Romans 8:5-6).

Then is disease always caused by sin? Not always. Just like the disciples' inquiry, there are many cases where a disease is caused by a sin that goes against God, but there are also exceptions.

There are cases where a person gets sick after eating the wrong type of food, or overexerting their body without exercising caution or self-control. Diseases may also come as a result of anxiety, mental stress, or demon-possession due to subjugation by Satan. There are also rare cases where a sperm or an egg with a defect becomes fertilized.

But most diseases or in-born disabilities occur because the person himself or his parent, and/or his ancestors committed idolatry and/or many other sins. However, the case of this blind man was a rare one. The man's blindness was not caused by some sin, but for the glory of God to be revealed through him.

Why Was He Blind From Birth?

"Jesus answered, 'It was neither that this man sinned, nor his parents; but it was so that the works of God might be displayed in him.'" (9:3)

To the disciples' inquiry, Jesus answered, "it was so that the works of God might be displayed in him." If we take this answer literally, it sounds like God purposely caused this man to be blind from birth. This is not the case though. Would a God so full of love that He sacrificed His only begotten Son to save the sinners purposely make someone blind from birth? No way! Then what did Jesus mean here?

In Luke chapter 4, there is a scene in which Jesus was handed and opened up the Book of Isaiah and read the prophecy of the Prophet Isaiah. This prophecy implicitly talks about Jesus' mission for coming to earth, and what kind of work He would be doing here. And, just as Isaiah's prophecy said, Jesus raised the dead, healed the sick, opened the eyes of the blind, and caused the mute speak.

When He began His public ministry, Jesus read the Scripture: *"The Spirit of the Lord is upon Me, because He anointed Me to preach the gospel to the poor. He has sent Me to proclaim release to the captives, and recovery of sight to the blind, to set free those who are oppressed, to proclaim the favorable year of the Lord"* (Luke 4:18-19).

The blind man also was chosen to display the glory of God. But he wasn't just chosen for no reason. This man came into this world as a result of a defective sperm and an egg that became fertilized. This did not occur because of a sin. But because of this handicap, he spent many days in turmoil, which earned him God's compassion. His confession and actions after being healed show us why he was chosen (John 9:17, 27).

"We must work the works of Him who sent Me as long as it is day; night is coming when no one can work. While I am in the world, I am the Light of the world." (9:4-5)

The Bible has many illustrations using night and day. 1 Thessalonians 5:5 says, *"For you are all sons of light and sons of day. We are not of night nor of darkness."* Romans 13:13 says, *"Let us behave properly as in the day, not in carousing and drunkenness, not in sexual promiscuity and sensuality, not in strife and jealousy."* So, according to the Bible, day symbolizes everything that is part of the truth, and night symbolizes darkness and all that is untruth.

Somewhat in retrospect, day is symbolic of the normal time to work. In this day and age, with the advancement of industry and technology, however, there are many people who work late-night shifts. But in Jesus' time, most people worked during the day time. So 'day' refers to the time for working, or the time to do God's work. And "the works of Him who sent Me", refers to the spiritual work of giving glory to God, and leading many people to believe in God.

So Jesus healed the blind man, giving glory to God and helping many people to believe in God. Just as our work comes to an end when the sun goes down and twilight covers the land, Jesus taught us that the end time will come, when we cannot do any more spiritual work for God. Here, the last days refers to Jesus' second coming.

Jesus said, "While I am in the world, I am the Light of the world." He said this because He came into this world to light up the darkness (Luke 2:32; John 1:4). Just as light chases away the darkness, the people who recognized Jesus realized, on their own, that they were sinners, and changed. And Jesus spread the gospel of Heaven, or the Words of truth, and performed signs and wonders (Matthew 4:23-24). To the sick, He became the Light of healing, to the suffering, He became the Light of peace, and to the whole world, He became the Light of truth, lighting up the path to Heaven.

Jesus Made Clay of the Spittle and Applied It to the Man's Eyes

"When He had said this, He spat on the ground, and made clay of the spittle, and applied the clay to his eyes, and said to him, 'Go, wash in the pool of Siloam' (which is translated, Sent) So he went away and washed, and came back seeing." (9:6-7)

After teaching His disciples with the truth, He began healing the blind man. He spat on the ground and made clay of the spittle and applied it to the man's eyes. Now there are some people who mistakenly think that Jesus used a worldly way to heal this man. They think that the clay was some healing material. However, Jesus even brought a dead man back to life with His single command. Why would He need to use a healing aid? Let alone, clay doesn't have anything in it that could heal someone's vision! The only reason Jesus used His spit was simply to make the clay.

But when healing the blind man at Bethsaida, Jesus actually spat directly onto the man's eyes (Mark 8:22-26). This has a spiritual significance. People think of spit as dirty. When someone spits at them, they consider that as a great insult. The reason why Jesus spat like this, was to help the man realize that his infirmity came from dirty sins and curses.

Then why did Jesus make clay of the spittle for the man who was blind from birth and put it on his eyes? This was in consideration of his faith. Some people can be encouraged simply with words to have stronger faith, but some people need to be given some visible evidence to have stronger faith.

Because this blind man never got to see any of the signs Jesus performed, it was difficult for him to have faith. Knowing this, Jesus wanted to encourage him in a way that would help him have more absolute faith and help him obey. Even though he couldn't see, if he felt something on his eyes, he could think, "Oh, maybe this will finally help me see," and have greater faith.

Now the case of blind man Bartimaeus at Jericho was a little different (Mark 10:46-52). He was healed simply by Jesus' Words. This was because his heart and his faith were like none other. Even though the people around him scolded him and told him to be quiet, he shouted earnestly and all the more loudly, *"Jesus, Son of David, have mercy on me!"* (v. 47) Throwing aside his cloak, which was everything he owned, he even put his faith into action and came out to Jesus. As a result, even though Jesus never put any clay on his eyes, his eyes were opened the instant Jesus said the words, *"Go; your faith has made you well"* (v. 52).

Compared to Bartimaeus, this blind man had little faith. This is why Jesus put the clay on his eyes to plant stronger faith in him, and then said, "Go, wash in the pool of Siloam." When he obeyed and went to the pool of Siloam and washed, an amazing thing took place! Everything became bright before his eyes, and he was able to see the light, and the beautiful world around him! It was a captivating moment for him, and he felt as if he was born again. He was living a life in the dark, without any hope. But when he met Jesus, his whole life turned around!

If he procrastinated in going to the pool of Siloam, or considered it a hassle and washed somewhere else, he probably would not have been healed. This is how important it is to obey and put your obedience into action (James 2:22). If water spiritually symbolizes the Word, then "the act of going and washing" symbolizes faith. Because he took faith and washed with the Word, he opened his eyes, and was able to see.

The Confession of the Blind Man

"Therefore the neighbors, and those who previously saw him as a beggar, were saying, 'Is not this the one who used to sit and beg?' Others were saying, 'This is he'; still others were saying, 'No, but he is like him.' He kept saying, 'I am the one.' So they were saying to him, 'How then were your eyes opened?' He answered, 'The man who is called Jesus made clay, and anointed my eyes, and said to me, "Go to Siloam and wash"; so I went away and washed, and I received sight.' They said to him, 'Where

: : The Pool of Siloam, whose waters are collected from the Gihon Spring

is He?' He said, 'I do not know.'" (9:8-12)

When the blind man was healed after meeting Jesus, people around him began talking in amazement. How marvelous it was that a man who had lived all of his life in the dark, begging to make a living, regained his sight and hope in life?! However, everyone around him showed different reactions.

The people who said "No, he was not the one who was blind," were the closed-minded ones. According to their own frame of mind, there was no way a blind man could receive sight. On the contrary, those people who said, "This is he," were the good-hearted ones, who acknowledged that he was healed. We can distinguish how much good a person has in his heart just by a few words that he says. The person who was blind became confounded by all the different reactions he received from people. And to the people who did not believe, he said, "I am the one," and he proudly identified himself.

Even today, when God's power is shown, there are people who show uncertainty and try to make sure it is true. With doubtful eyes, they try to seek out some fallacy. One by one, people began crowding around, asking, "How then were your eyes opened?"

They weren't simply asking to find out what method was used to heal him. They were trying to find something wrong in the situation, because in their minds, they were thinking, "There's no way a blind man can come to see!" So, naturally, the man who was healed felt as if he had done something wrong, and began feeling intimidated. Now normally, when put in this kind of situation, people lie or say this and that to avoid confrontation or a negative experience of some sort. However, this man had a true heart, so he honestly explained exactly how he became healed. He said, "The man who is called Jesus made clay, and anointed my eyes, and said to me, 'Go to Siloam and wash'; so I went away and washed, and I received sight."

But the people's reactions were not all that positive. Instead of rejoicing for him, they asked where Jesus was. And the day that Jesus healed the blind man happened to be the Sabbath day (John 9:14). The Jews considered opening the eyes of a blind man as a type of labor, and they thought that Jesus broke the Sabbath. Only then, did the man realize what was going on, and thinking that Jesus might get in trouble because of him, he quickly told the people that he didn't know where He was.

The Blind Man Who Was Healed and the Pharisees

The Pharisees greatly valued the Law of Moses; to the point they could memorize every word. However, they only dwelled on the formality of the Law, and because Jesus healed the sick on the Sabbath day, they treated Him as a sinner. According to their standard, yes, Jesus broke the Sabbath, but Jesus only did good works, works that brought souls to life. And this was because Jesus actually understood the depths of God's heart, who gave us the Law in the first place.

The Pharisees' Dispute

"They brought to the Pharisees the man who was formerly blind. Now it was a Sabbath on the day when

Jesus made the clay and opened his eyes. Then the Pharisees also were asking him again how he received his sight. And he said to them, 'He applied clay to my eyes, and I washed, and I see.' Therefore some of the Pharisees were saying, 'This man is not from God, because He does not keep the Sabbath.' But others were saying, 'How can a man who is a sinner perform such signs?' And there was a division among them." (9:13-16)

The people who were feeling animosity toward Jesus took the healed man to the Pharisees. They had evidence that Jesus broke the Sabbath, but they themselves alone could not cross-examine Him or accuse Him of this offense. They needed someone with higher authority and power. When the Pharisees again asked the man how he came to see, he explained once again, the whole process of how he became healed. When people are struck with questions like this a second time, they become shaken, and they either change what they said the first time, or give a less detailed answer toward the end. However, he did not bend the truth. So in the end, opposing opinions over the point 'This man is not from God, because He does not keep the Sabbath' caused a great dispute among the Pharisees.

The reason they condemned Jesus was because according to the formality and procedures recorded in the Law, He broke the Sabbath. When the Pharisees talk about the Law, they are talking about the Pentateuch of Moses and the tradition of the elders which were passed down from generation to generation by word of mouth. This is why Jesus scolded them as being 'hypocrites' and 'whitewashed tombs' (Matthew 2:37). But on the other hand, there were people who raised an objection to everyone else's argument.

"How can a man who is a sinner perform such signs?" they asked. There were among the Pharisees, a few men with goodness in their hearts who argued and questioned how a sinner could perform signs. Yes, Jesus broke the Sabbath according to their standards, but they had to acknowledge that He did something that is humanly impossible to do.

The Jews Question the Parents of the Man Who Was Healed

"So they said to the blind man again, 'What do you say about Him, since He opened your eyes?' And he said, 'He is a prophet.' The Jews then did not believe it of him, that he had been blind and had received sight, until they called the parents of the very one who had received his sight, and questioned them, saying, 'Is this your son, who you say was born blind? Then how does he now see?'" (9:17-19)

As the dispute continued with people reasoning and arguing about what is right, and what is wrong, someone threw a question at the man who was healed saying, "What do you say about Him?"

All eyes were on him. Depending on his answer, the Pharisees' anger could become aroused even more, or it could subside. He answered without hesitation.

"He is a prophet."

He believed that unless this man was of God, He could not have healed his eyes. In reality, Jesus did not come into this world as a prophet, but the Messiah, or the Christ, but to him who did not know this truth yet, he wanted to call Jesus whatever name he could give that showed his utmost honor and respect.

But because of this answer, the negative emotions that the Pharisees had against Jesus became deeper. Even after hearing the healed man's clear answer, the Jews did not accept it. They finally called the man's parents and began questioning them and saying, "Is this your son, who you say was born blind? Then how does he now see?" His parents, who were called abruptly before the Pharisees, didn't know what to do. They were afraid something bad may happen to them, and they became very nervous.

"He Is of Age, Ask Him."

"His parents answered them and said, 'We know that this is our son, and that he was born blind; but how he now sees, we do not know; or who opened his eyes, we do not know. Ask him; he is of age, he will speak for himself.' His parents said this because they were afraid of the Jews; for the Jews had already agreed that if anyone confessed Him to be Christ, he was to be put out of the synagogue. For this reason his parents said,

'He is of age; ask him.'" (9:20-23)

The parents confirm that their son was born blind. However, because they feared the Jews, they couldn't truthfully say any more, and they avoided answering the question by turning the responsibility over to their son. "But how he now sees, we do not know; or who opened his eyes, we do not know. Ask him; he is of age, he will speak for himself."

There was a reason the parents tried to avoid answering the question. The Jews had decided that anyone who confessed that Jesus was the Christ would be put out of the synagogue. To "put someone out of the synagogue" means to cut off a person's ties with the synagogues and expel him or her for committing some wrongdoing.

Depending on the seriousness of the wrongdoing, there are three types of punishment a person can receive.

The first type is where the person is severely rebuked by a person of religious authority, and then he is deprived of all religious rights for 7-30 days.

The second type is where the person is banned from all social gatherings for at least 30 days. If this form of penalty is ineffective, the third type is enforced.

The third type is where the person is indefinitely deprived of all religious privileges. When a person receives this form of punishment, for the rest of his life, the person will be isolated and scorned by people; and his house, work, and even his life may be threatened.

So 'being put out of the synagogue' means losing everything. So the parents of the man who was healed were gripped with the fear of possibly receiving this kind of punishment. Being pressed by the Jews' intimidating words, they left the task of answering the question to their son.

As parents of a son who was blind since birth, how do you think they felt? They probably spent many a day feeling very sad and sorry for their son. And now that he came to see, they should have been grateful to Jesus for the rest of their lives! But as soon as they realized that their lives could be in danger, they avoided the truth in a cowardly manner. Even though their son was in a situation where he could be harmed, they shifted the responsibility over to him. This is what fleshly love is; seeking after the benefit of one's own self first.

"You do not want to become His disciples too, do you?"

"So a second time they called the man who had been blind, and said to him, 'Give glory to God; we know that this man is a sinner.' He then answered, 'Whether He is a sinner, I do not know; one thing I do know, that though I was blind, now I see.' So they said to him, 'What did He do to you? How did He open your eyes?'

He answered them, 'I told you already and you did not listen; why do you want to hear it again? You do not want to become His disciples too, do you?'" (9:24-27)

When the parents of the healed man did not give them an answer, the Pharisees called the man again and told him to give glory to God. Since they are a people who have been worshipping God generation after generation, of course they will give glory to God in any event. Then why did the Pharisees tell the man to "give glory to God" in such a blatant way? To them, it wasn't really about God. They were concerned that as the man continued to praise Jesus, whom they hated, more people would begin following Him.

The Pharisees told the man to just give glory to God, because they thought Jesus was a sinner. However, this is contrary to reason. How could a sinner open the eyes of a blind man and thereby give glory to God? No matter how you look at it, this was just wrong. From the healed man's perspective, these people were telling him that the man who healed him and gave him new life and hope was a sinner, so how stifling this whole situation was! So the man tried to tell them indirectly that Jesus was a man of God. "Whether He is a sinner, I do not know; one thing I do know, that though I was blind, now I see."

Rather than trying to confront the people who were calling Jesus a sinner by saying, "No, He's not," the man pointed out the truth, which served as a more clear and effective argument. This man did not cower to persecution or threats. He had a true heart, so he did not forget the grace he received. That is why even though he did not ask Jesus to open his eyes, Jesus came to him and healed him.

When the Pharisees did not receive the answer they wanted, instead of getting rid of their sinister motives, they continued to find some way to accuse Jesus as a sinner. So they kept questioning the man, "What did He do to you? How did He open your eyes?"

These questions were not questions that asked for the truth. These questions came from the Pharisees' evil intentions. Because they did not believe in any work related to Jesus, they wanted to find some reason to confront Jesus. But the man who was healed of his blindness did not avoid, or grow weary of answering these double-edged questions. "I told you already and you did not listen; why do you want to hear it again? You do not want to become His disciples too, do you?"

The man wondered, "I told them everything. That should be enough to help them understand. I wonder why they are asking me again?" He couldn't figure out what their intentions were, so he thought maybe they also wanted to become disciples of Jesus. Because he had a good heart, he took their evil questions in a positive way.

The Pharisees Reviled the Blind Man Who Was Healed

"They reviled him and said, 'You are His disciple, but we are disciples of Moses. We know that God has spoken to Moses, but as for this man, we do not know where He is from.' The man answered and said to them,

'Well, here is an amazing thing, that you do not know where He is from, and yet He opened my eyes.'" (9:28-30)

The healed man's kind words ultimately stirred up more anger among the Pharisees. They raised their voice, saying, "You are His disciple, but we are disciples of Moses. We know that God has spoken to Moses, but as for this man, we do not know where He is from."

On the surface, the Pharisees taught the Law of Moses, so they could argue that they were disciples of Moses. However, they did not obey the Law with their hearts. If they were true disciples of Moses, then they should have recognized Jesus and given glory to God. By claiming to have a relationship with Moses, who received the Law directly from God, they tried to claim that their words were righteous. This is sort of like someone showing off about one of their famous ancestors and bluffing about themselves.

The man who was once blind was not very learned, and he possessed nothing; but he knew that what the Pharisees were saying didn't make much sense. What made him even more puzzled was that these men had knowledge incomparable to himself, and they were in the position of teaching all of their people; and yet they did not recognize Jesus. He just could not understand saying, "Well, here is an amazing thing, that you do not know where He is from, and yet He opened my eyes."

Although he didn't have much knowledge, and nobody taught him, because he was a good man of truth, he knew what was true. Even though he wasn't an expert of the laws or the traditions of the elders, he could spiritually feel what kind of a man Jesus was, and he realized who He was. Even though he just experienced God, and didn't know much about His work, the reason why he gained spiritual enlightenment so quickly, was because that's how clean his heart was.

Even today, just like the Pharisees, we may have piled up a lot of knowledge about our faith and spirituality, and we may even look holy on the outside, but there are cases where what we know may very well become our framework, or the very thing that cages us. Even within the same Christian community, because doctrines and denominations become frameworks, people argue, "This is right, or this is wrong," and divisions are created, and there are cases where people condemn one another. For example, the Bible says, "Cry out in prayer". But if people in a certain church pray out loud and cry out in prayer, people say, "That's a strange church." And when healing takes place in a church, some people say, "That church is into mysticism." Basically, these people are judging God's work based on rules and regulations created by man.

The Steadfast Heart of the Blind Man Who Was Healed

"'We know that God does not hear sinners; but if anyone is God-fearing and does His will, He hears him. Since the beginning of time it has never been heard that anyone opened the eyes of a person born blind. If this man were not from God, He could do nothing.' They

answered him, 'You were born entirely in sins, and are you teaching us?' So they put him out." (9:31-34)

Imagine the scene where the blind man who was healed is surrounded by men filled with evil, being interrogated by them. The man had to be shaking with fear. Each word they threw at him was thorny, and probably came across as near threats. All the men standing before him were men born of elite families, respected by society; men of reputation and class. On the other hand, he was a mere beggar who begged on the streets for a living. But he did not become intimidated by their oppressing and formidable presence. He told the truth until the bitter end. What a steadfast heart he had!

The man also confessed that since the beginning of time, this was the first time that the eyes of a man born blind were opened. Here, the fact that Jesus opened the eyes of a blind man has a great spiritual significance. It signifies that Jesus not only has the power to simply perform a sign, but that He also has the power to open spiritual eyes as well.

Spiritually, all mankind is born blind. But by believing in Jesus Christ, our spiritual eyes are opened, and we come to see the spiritual world, and Heaven. The fact that the eyes of the man born blind became opened by Jesus, is a foreshadowing of this spiritual significance.

Just as the healed man said, how can a man not from God open the eyes of a blind man? Only a god who has greater power than man can do such a thing. No matter how much science and technology develops, this is something man just cannot do. This is one of those things that only God's power can do. That is why the healed man testified that Jesus came from God. However, the Pharisees did not listen to him to the end.

Being Spiritually Blind

Word about the blind man's eyes being opened, and about the blind man being put out by the Pharisees spread rapidly. In order to give the man greater blessings than the blessing he had already received when he was healed, Jesus met the man one more time. And the reason Jesus came up to the man first and met him twice—not just once—is apparent in the man's actions thus far.

"Do You Believe in the Son of Man?"

"Jesus heard that they had put him out, and finding him, He said, 'Do you believe in the Son of Man?' He answered, 'Who is He, Lord, that I may believe in

Him?' Jesus said to him, 'You have both seen Him, and He is the one who is talking with you.' And he said, 'Lord, I believe.' And he worshiped Him." (9:35-38)

Jesus met the blind man who was healed, and asked, "Do you believe in the Son of Man?" What He means by this is, "Do you believe in God's Son, the Messiah, who forgave your sins and saved you?" The man did not know that the one who opened his eyes was the Messiah his people had so long been waiting for. He simply thought He was someone from God. "Who is He, Lord, that I may believe in Him?"

So in reply he said he wanted to believe in the Son of God who forgave his sins and who will lead him to salvation. He was confessing that although he didn't know until now, he wants to believe. Knowing the man's heart, Jesus revealed that He was the Messiah who opened his eyes when He said, "You have both seen Him, and He is the one who is talking with you." The man who had been blind replied, "Lord, I believe."

Jesus didn't say much, but the man understood. He bowed and worshipped before Jesus and confessed his faith. Worshiping is an act that shows utmost respect and gratitude. The man believed that Jesus was the Messiah, not simply with his lips, but with his heart.

The Pharisees, Who Were Spiritually Blind

"And Jesus said, 'For judgment I came into this

world, so that those who do not see may see, and that those who see may become blind.' "Those of the Pharisees who were with Him heard these things and said to Him, 'We are not blind too, are we?' "Jesus said to them, 'If you were blind, you would have no sin; but since you say, "We see," your sin remains.'" (9:39-41)

Jesus told Nicodemus, who came to Him at night, *"For God did not send the Son into the world to judge the world, but that the world might be saved through Him"* (John 3:17). But in this passage, Jesus said, "For judgment I came into this world." This may seem like Jesus is contradicting Himself, but He is not. He is telling them exactly what "judgment" means, according to God. Jesus' ultimate goal for coming to this world is to save us, not to judge us and send us to Hell. However, those people who do not believe ultimately have to receive judgment, because the wages of sin is death (Romans 6:23).

What did Jesus mean when He said, "For judgment I came into this world, so that those who do not see may see, and that those who see may become blind"? When we compare the blind man to the Pharisees, we can understand what this means. Even though someone may be physically blind, if his heart seeks God, and he is a good person, he will recognize the Messiah and receive salvation and eternal life. However, like the Pharisees, someone may have two eyes that can see physically well, but if his spiritual eyes are blinded by the evil in his heart, he cannot receive salvation. The Pharisees who were with Jesus asked Him, "We are not blind too, are we?"

They were confronting Jesus because He said, "Those who

see may become blind." They were not asking this question because they really didn't know. Since they could see, they wanted to point out that they were not blind. The Pharisees just did not understand Jesus' Words. Seeing their reaction, Jesus was heartbroken. "If you were blind, you would have no sin; but since you say, 'We see,' your sin remains."

If someone is blind, we can assume that he does not know because he cannot see. But the Pharisees were not blind. They spent so much time studying and teaching the laws, and yet they did not understand. That's why Jesus said, "Your sin remains."

Chapter *10*

"I Am the Good Shepherd"

The Parable
of the Good Shepherd

The mountainous country of Israel has many steep slopes and rocks, so one must take extra caution of their surroundings when raising sheep in that region. The nearby plains are not very grassy, so shepherds must travel long distances tending their sheep. A good shepherd will spare no effort to lead his sheep to green pastures and quiet waters. Jesus often taught spiritual truths using illustrations that people could easily connect with, and the sheep and the shepherd were among the most frequently used illustrations in Jesus' teachings.

The Sheep and the Shepherd

"Truly, truly, I say to you, he who does not enter by

the door into the fold of the sheep, but climbs up some other way, he is a thief and a robber. But he who enters by the door is a shepherd of the sheep." (10:1-2)

During the day, the shepherd moves around in search of a good pasture for his sheep. When the day comes to an end, he takes his sheep to a safe pen. A cave or a wall of stones could be used as a pen. In the case of a shepherd using a cave as the pen, he would set up a small door a few feet in front of the entrance to the cave, and he piles stones on both sides of the door to cover the entrance to the cave. The entrance is very narrow, and he plants thorns above it to keep the wolves and the thieves out. Of course the shepherd who tends the sheep will enter and exit through the door of the pen. If someone enters the pen by climbing over the wall, then he is most likely to try to steal the sheep.

Why would Jesus tell us something so obvious? This is because the sheep, the shepherd, the pen, the door, the thief, and the robber symbolize something that is spiritually significant. First, the "sheep" symbolizes God's children. A new believer who has just accepted Jesus, or a believer of many years, a believer with big faith, a believer with little faith—any person who received salvation is considered a "sheep". The "sheep pen" symbolizes a place where the sheep gather to rest; in other words, the "pen" is the church where God's children can gather to receive true Sabbath and peace.

In 1 Corinthians 1:2 it describes, *"To the church of God which is at Corinth, to those who have been sanctified in Christ Jesus, saints by calling, with all who in every place call on the name of our Lord Jesus Christ, their Lord and ours.* " A church both signifies a type of building, and all the believers. So the sheep pen can also signify the gathering of God's children. Just as Jesus said in John 10:7, *"I am the door of the sheep,"* the door symbolizes Jesus Christ.

Then who does the "shepherd of the sheep" symbolize? Hebrews 13:20 says, *"Now the God of peace, who brought up from the dead the great Shepherd of the sheep through the blood of the eternal covenant, even Jesus our Lord"* and 1 Peter 5:4 says, *"And when the Chief Shepherd appears, you will receive the unfading crown of glory."* So we can see that Jesus Christ is both the "Great Shepherd" and the "Chief Shepherd."

Let's suppose there were ten thousand sheep. If we divide the sheep into ten groups, and appoint one shepherd per group, then a chief shepherd will preside over the ten shepherds. Spiritually, the Lord Jesus is the Chief Shepherd. And God's servants are appointed by God for each of His churches, and all the servants who take care of the souls within the church, can be called the "shepherds."

Lastly, who then are the "thief and robbers"? Anyone who leads the believers astray by calling himself God or the resurrected Christ; the antichrist, who denies that Jesus Christ came into this world in the flesh; and any heretical cult that denies the Lord who ransomed us by paying the penalty of our sins is the "thief" and the "robber" (2 Peter 2:1).

The Sheep Who Hear the Shepherd's Voice

> "To him the doorkeeper opens, and the sheep hear
> his voice, and he calls his own sheep by name and leads
> them out. When he puts forth all his own, he goes
> ahead of them, and the sheep follow him because they
> know his voice. A stranger they simply will not follow,
> but will flee from him, because they do not know the
> voice of strangers. This figure of speech Jesus spoke to
> them, but they did not understand what those things
> were which He had been saying to them." (10:3-6)

When morning comes, the shepherd stands at the door and
calls the names of his sheep in order to take them to a place
with water and pasture. The sheep, which rested peacefully
under the protection of the shepherd, hear his voice and come
out of the pen. What would happen if someone else put on the
shepherd's clothes and tried to imitate the shepherd's voice?
They say the sheep recognize the difference and try to flee.
Using these special characteristics of sheep as an illustration,
Jesus gave a spiritual teaching.

Now the "doorkeeper" who opens the door for the shepherd
is the Holy Spirit. To anyone who accepts Jesus Christ, God
gives him the Holy Spirit as a gift. The Holy Spirit, who resides
in us, helps us communicate with God and live according to
God's Word. So when the Scripture says, "the doorkeeper
opens the door for the shepherd", it is referring to these roles of
the Holy Spirit. And the "door" in this verse is different from
the "door" mentioned in the earlier verses. The "door" here

symbolizes the door of our thoughts and hearts, as children of God.

Just as sheep can accurately distinguish their shepherd's voice from other voices, a believer who received the Holy Spirit can also distinguish the voice of the Lord. In the truth, a person can clearly recognize if other servants of the Lord are one with the Chief Shepherd or not. When the Jews could not understand the spiritual significance within these illustrations, Jesus explained again, applying the concept to Himself.

"I Am the Door of the Sheep"

"So Jesus said to them again, 'Truly, truly, I say to you, I am the door of the sheep. All who came before Me are thieves and robbers, but the sheep did not hear them.'" (10:7-8)

In order to understand why Jesus said He was the "door of the sheep", we need to go back to the time of the Exodus, which took place 400 years after the Israelites' ancestor, Jacob, and his whole family moved and settled in Egypt to avoid the famine.

When Jacob's family, which originally consisted of about 70 people, grew so much in number that they could be called a "nation", to the Egyptian Pharaoh they had become a threat. That's why he turned them into slaves and began persecuting them. Harsh labor was hard enough to withstand, but as the Pharaoh's abuse grew worse and worse, the people of Israel cried out to God to save them.

So God chose Moses to tell the Pharaoh to let the Israelites go, but the Pharaoh didn't let them go very easily. As the Pharaoh began changing his words and going against God's will, the nation of Egypt received all kinds of plagues. They began with the plague of blood, then frogs, lice, flies, livestock, boils, hail, locusts, and even the plague of darkness. The whole country was becoming exhausted. And the whole time the Egyptians were experiencing all these plagues, the Israelites were protected by God.

Right before the last plague—the plague where the firstborn of every Egyptian family, and the firstborn of every animal died—God told the people of Israel how to stay safe from this plague. He told them to slaughter a young lamb at twilight and put the blood on the tops and sides of the doorframes of their house, roast the meat over the fire, and eat it, staying inside the house. The sides of the doorframes are pillars that support the door, and the tops are supports made of wood or stone that lay horizontally above the door to hold up the wall. In the pitch-dark night, the shadow of death did not go to the houses of the Israelites who obeyed God and put the blood of the young lamb on the doorframes of their houses.

Here, the blood of the young lamb spiritually signifies the blood of Jesus Christ. Just as the shadow of death did not go to the houses with the blood on its doorframes, anyone who believes the fact that Jesus died on the cross and shed His blood, and by His blood we were forgiven of our sins will escape from death and go to eternal life. Even though they did not know this spiritual meaning behind what they did, they were saved from the last plague.

But households that did not put the blood of the lamb on the sides and tops of their doorframes experienced the death of their firstborn sons. And some who had put the blood on the doorframes were still not able to evade the shadow of death because they didn't stay inside the house as God instructed them to do. This is symbolic of someone who accepted the Lord but lost their salvation because they once again left the framework or boundaries of salvation. Just as the Israelites were saved only when they put the blood of the lamb on the sides and tops of their doorframes and stayed inside the house, we can only be saved if we stay in Jesus Christ, who saved us by shedding His blood for our sins. This is why Jesus said, "I am the door of the sheep."

Jesus also said, "All who came before Me are thieves and robbers." Who could Jesus be talking about here? The words "came before" in this verse doesn't just refer to some time before. The time that Jesus came into this world to save mankind from their sins had already been appointed by God's providence. He came approximately 2,000 years ago, at the most appropriate time to carry out God's will. At that time, the prosperity of the Roman Empire was such that people even now commonly use the phrase "All roads lead to Rome." The prosperity of the Roman Empire and the development of the Hellenistic civilization served greatly as a mechanism in quickly spreading the gospel of Jesus Christ to the whole world.

If anyone had appeared and said, "I am the Christ," without the related timing, then it was a lie. The same goes for the Lord's Second Coming. God's appointed time has no room for even a slight margin of error. If someone comes at a time that's different from this set time and says, "I am the Christ," or another says, "This is the way to salvation," then these people are thieves and robbers.

"If Anyone Enters Through Me"

"I am the door; if anyone enters through Me, he will be saved, and will go in and out and find pasture. The thief comes only to steal and kill and destroy; I came that they may have life, and have it abundantly." (10:9-10)

Anyone who believes in, and follows Jesus Christ—the door of the sheep—will not only receive salvation, but whenever he comes in and goes out, he will also receive nourishment. But the clause, "if anyone enters through Me," is an absolute prerequisite. Only when a person lives according to the Word of the Lord, who is the truth itself, can that person then receive salvation and blessings. When we listen to God's Word and live according to it, God promises to set us 'high above all the nations of the earth' and we will be blessed 'when we come in and blessed when we go out' (Deuteronomy 28:1-14).

On the contrary, who are the people who are compared to the "thief"? They pretend to be the Christ, and they tell others to follow them in order to receive salvation. But at the end of that road, is death. So the thief comes to steal and kill, but Jesus came to give us life, and life abundant. Just as it is written in 3 John 1:2, when our soul prospers, we have good health, and all goes well for us. Jesus came so we may have this kind of life. When the Scripture says our "soul prospers", it means that our heart is filled with the truth. And when our heart is filled with the truth, our actions will clearly show it. We will be able to obey God's Words completely, we will rejoice always, pray continuously, and give thanks in all circumstances. When we do this, the enemy devil and Satan will flee from us, and all trials, tribulations, and illnesses will flee with them, so we can receive the blessing of good health.

The Good Shepherd and the Hired Hand

"I am the good shepherd; the good shepherd lays down His life for the sheep. He who is a hired hand, and not a shepherd, who is not the owner of the sheep, sees the wolf coming, and leaves the sheep and flees, and the wolf snatches them and scatters them. He flees because he is a hired hand and is not concerned about the sheep." (10:11-13)

King David was a shepherd when he was a young man. When herding sheep, there are times when lions or bears come and run off with a sheep or two. But whenever this happened, David chased down the predator, killed it, and saved the sheep. Jesus talked to the Jews using this as an illustration. The good shepherd would fight off the predator, even at the risk his own life, to save the sheep's life. However, if a hired hand's life is in danger, he will abandon the sheep and flee for his life. So we can differentiate between a good shepherd and a hired hand by looking at the fruit that they bear (Matthew 7:17).

Because Jesus would not even spare His own life when He became the atoning sacrifice for man's sins, He could save mankind from going the way of death. Jesus took the suffering on the cross in order to lead us in the way of salvation. He is the only 'good' shepherd and the one true shepherd. Unlike the Lord who served us with His whole life, the hired hand wants to be served by others. The hired hand does whatever he can to flaunt himself and make himself known. If something doesn't sit right with him, he harbors negative emotions and brings about enmity. If he is in a situation that doesn't benefit himself, or he faces some kind of hardship, he flees; looking for a way to save himself.

"I Lay Down My Life for the Sheep"

"I am the good shepherd, and I know My own and My own know Me, even as the Father knows Me and I know the Father; and I lay down My life for the sheep." (10:14-15)

The good shepherd knows when his sheep are hungry and when he has to feed them. He feeds them, puts them to sleep on time, and he protects them from harm, so his sheep grow strong and healthy. A diligent shepherd knows exactly what condition each sheep is in, and he provides an effective solution to any problems that may arise for the sheep. And using this as an illustration, Jesus said, "I know My own and My own know Me."

What does it mean to know someone, according to this Scripture? It means to know the souls that God entrusted to us: not only their name, family background, family situation, and work, which pertain to their physical conditions, but their spiritual condition as well. We should know if the souls entrusted to us are getting enough spiritual nourishment, and make sure they're not malnourished, and we must check to see if they have any illnesses. And it is not enough to simply know the problem. If a person does not have faith, we must help them to have faith. If a person has sin, we must help him realize what his sins are and help him live in righteousness. If a person doesn't know how to pray, we need to help him to pray. These are the responsibilities of a good shepherd.

We can see the heart of a truly good shepherd in the confession of the apostle Paul, *"I have been in labor and hardship, through many sleepless nights, in hunger and thirst, often without food, in cold and exposure. Apart from such external things, there is the daily pressure on me of concern for all the churches. Who is weak without my being weak? Who is led into sin without my intense concern?"* (2 Corinthians 11:27-29)

When a shepherd has this kind of heart and takes sincere care of his sheep, giving them correct prescriptions and teachings, the sheep will naturally love and trust their shepherd. Because they love their shepherd, they will listen to his voice and follow him. As the good shepherd, Jesus came to call the sinners and lead them to repentance, so He helps the sinners realize their sins, cast out those sins, and live in the midst of righteousness. He teaches the truth according to each person's measure of faith and gives him strength and hope to live according to the Word.

"I Lay It Down on My Own Initiative"

"I have other sheep, which are not of this fold; I must bring them also, and they will hear My voice; and they will become one flock with one shepherd. For this reason the Father loves Me, because I lay down My life so that I may take it again. No one has taken it away from Me, but I lay it down on My own initiative I have authority to lay it down, and I have authority to take it up again. This commandment I received from My Father." (10:16-18)

As it is written in Luke 5:32, *"I have not come to call the righteous but sinners to repentance,"* Jesus' mission for coming to this world was to save many souls who are not within the boundaries of salvation. When Jesus says, "I have other sheep, which are not of this fold," He is talking about the people who do not believe in God and have not accepted Jesus Christ. Jesus is saying that these people must be led to Him and become a part of the holy flock; in other words, believers.

Therefore children of God who are already saved must

spread the gospel. As commanded by Jesus Christ in Acts 1:8, *"But you will receive power when the Holy Spirit has come upon you; and you shall be My witnesses both in Jerusalem, and in all Judea and Samaria, and even to the remotest part of the earth,"* whether or not we have the time, we must make the time and make every effort to work for the cause of spreading the gospel.

The reason Jesus laid down His life was to save us and lead us to Heaven. He did not lay down His life reluctantly just because it was God's will. Just like a child who loves and understands his parents' heart and voluntarily obeys their will, Jesus obeyed with joy. Jesus knew, better than anyone else, the sorrow in God's heart for the souls who were going toward eternal death.

That is why Jesus chose the road that led to laying down His life. Although at the end of this road was glory, this road was not an easy one; it was a continuation of suffering. But He voluntarily chose to take up this charge, so how joyful must God have been! How lovely Jesus must have looked to God! So that is why He bestowed His power upon Jesus, and He showed Him even greater works that all would see and marvel at (John 5:20). The signs, wonders, and works of amazing power that were displayed through Jesus are evidence of God's love for Jesus.

God also gave us the authority to become His children. It is as written in Mark 16:17, *"These signs will accompany those who have believed,"* God promises us that as His children, as long as we have the pure faith, He will be with us through signs, just as He was with Jesus.

The Jews' Dispute

"A division occurred again among the Jews because of these words. Many of them were saying, 'He has a demon and is insane. Why do you listen to Him?' Others were saying, 'These are not the sayings of one demon-possessed. A demon cannot open the eyes of the blind, can he?'" (10:19-21)

Instead of rejoicing and giving thanks with the blind man who was healed, the Jews got into a dispute among themselves and then finally forced the man to leave. And after hearing Jesus' illustration about the sheep and the shepherd in an attempt to enlighten them, another argument arose. After people began accusing Jesus of being demon-possessed, they began quarreling with one another. Some said, "He has a demon and is insane. Why do you listen to Him?" while others said, "These are not the sayings of one demon-possessed. A demon cannot open the eyes of the blind, can he?"

Their heated disagreement and dispute steadily escalated until they finally decided to 'kill' Jesus. Fundamentally, their hearts were evil, so they did not hesitate to condemn others and they did not refrain from speaking and acting out of evil. They called themselves the people of God, and they were in the position of studying and teaching the Law. But because their eyes were blinded from the truth, they accused Jesus of being insane and demon-possessed even though they saw all the works of God that were manifested through Jesus Christ.

But not everyone judged and condemned Jesus out of the

evil. There were some among them with good hearts, who asked how a demon could open the eyes of a blind man. These people believed and accepted the works of Jesus as the manifestation of God's power. There is no way a demon could have the power to open the eyes of a blind man.

In the Bible we see people who become mute and deaf due to demon-possession. Demons bring illnesses, calamities, temptations, tribulations, and sufferings. Demons don't have anything to do with good works, such as opening the eyes of a blind man so that he could give glory to God (Mark 9:25; Luke 6:18, 9:42). Opening the blind man's eyes was the work of God, and He does this kind of work through His chosen people with whom He is pleased (Psalm 146:8; Judges 42:1-7).

"I and the Father Are One"

Just like any nation, the nation of Israel has special holidays. The three great holidays of the Jewish people are: the Passover, the Feast of Weeks, and the Feast of Tabernacles. Besides these holidays there are other holidays such as Rosh Hashanah, Yom Kippur, Purim, and the Feast of Dedication (Hanukkah).

Of these holidays, the Feast of Dedication, otherwise known as 'Hanukkah', is a holiday that commemorates the rededication of the Holy Temple. In 165 B.C., Jewish leader Maccabeus took back Jerusalem from Syria and rededicated the temple in Jerusalem, which was destroyed when Jerusalem was seized. To commemorate this event, the Jews celebrate Hanukkah to this day. From September 25 of the Jewish calendar (around December), for about eight days, the Jews celebrate with festivities. It is approximately the same time as

Christmas, which celebrates the birth of Jesus. The Jews do not acknowledge Jesus as the Christ, and celebrate Hanukkah instead.

"If You Are the Christ, Tell Us Plainly"

> "At that time the Feast of the Dedication took place at Jerusalem; it was winter, and Jesus was walking in the temple in the portico of Solomon. The Jews then gathered around Him, and were saying to Him, 'How long will You keep us in suspense? If You are the Christ, tell us plainly.'" (10:22-24)

It was the time of the Feast of Dedication. It was winter; and since Jesus took up the suffering on the cross in April of the following year, this was His last winter on earth. Around the time of the Feast of Dedication, Jesus was in the temple in the portico of Solomon. Located along the outer walls of the temple, the portico of Solomon didn't have any walls to block out the wind. Now if we look at a church, there is the church building, the church yard, and then the church fence. If we were to compare the temple to a church, the portico of Solomon would be like the church fence, located outside of the temple building. This location was often used by Rabbis who taught their disciples there.

Jesus and His disciples also went there to share the gospel, teach, heal sicknesses, and show God's power to the people. One day, a group of Jews came and gathered around Jesus as if they plotted to do so, and they randomly began asking Him questions such as, "How long will You keep us in suspense?" and "If You are the Christ, tell us plainly!"

The Jews expected Jesus to become intimidated by their presence and say that He was not the Christ. They did this because they did not acknowledge Jesus as God's Son, and considered Him as a mere person. They themselves were Israel's leaders with names and power. They were those who had thorough knowledge of the Law. To them, Jesus just looked like the son of a poor carpenter who went around with fishermen as disciples. That is why even though Jesus showed them plenty of signs and wonders to give them evidence to see and believe, they refused to believe. So how did Jesus respond to these people who demanded that He tell them plainly if He was the Christ?

"You Do Not Believe Because You Are Not of My Sheep"

> "Jesus answered them, 'I told you, and you do not believe; the works that I do in My Father's name, these testify of Me. But you do not believe because you are not of My sheep. My sheep hear My voice, and I know them, and they follow Me.'" (10:25-27).

God used many different ways to show that Jesus was the Savior. He told the people through John the Baptist. Jesus Himself told them. And through all the powerful works that were done in God's name He also testified to Himself. But the Jews did not acknowledge Him to the end.

"I told you, and you do not believe; the works that I do in My Father's name, these testify of Me."

The Jews not only refused to believe; they judged, condemned, and plotted how they could kill Jesus. However, just as a sheep knows its shepherd's voice and follows him, children of God should be able to believe all the things that God does through Jesus Christ.

"I and the Father Are One"

"And I give eternal life to them, and they will never perish; and no one will snatch them out of My hand. My Father, who has given them to Me, is greater than all; and no one is able to snatch them out of the Father's hand. I and the Father are one." (10:28-30)

Jesus said, "I give eternal life to them," because those who believe Jesus as the Savior receive the Holy Spirit; and their spirit, which was once dead, comes back to life. When the Holy Spirit gives birth to the spirit and as we begin to live in the Word of God more and more, then little by little we are changed by the truth. This is the way of eternal life. Because there is no death in Jesus Christ who has eternal life, when we believe in Him, we can have true life. Therefore, we do not perish, and we can enjoy true happiness for eternity in Heaven.

Jesus also said, "No one will snatch them out of My hand." This is a passage that shows how much Jesus loves us. What Jesus means in this passage is that since His sheep were entrusted to Him by God, He loves His sheep with His life; and no matter what dangers may come, He will not give up His sheep. So no one can take the sheep from Jesus' hands. *"Who will separate us from the love of Christ? Will tribulation, or distress, or persecution, or famine, or nakedness, or peril, or sword?"* (Romans 8:35).

On top of it all, God is greater than anything in creation. "Anything in creation" means all things that exist in the universe. The universe itself is unimaginably vast. Then who can grasp us from the hands of God, who is even greater than the vast universe? So after emphasizing that no one can take us away from Jesus as long as we believe follow Him, He tells us why this is so saying, "I and the Father are one."

The reason Jesus and God are one is because Jesus is the Word (God) that became flesh and came to this world (John 1:14). And just the fact that Jesus was conceived by the Holy Spirit lets us know that He is one with God.

The Jews Try to Stone Jesus

"The Jews picked up stones again to stone Him. Jesus answered them, 'I showed you many good works from the Father; for which of them are you stoning Me?' The Jews answered Him, 'For a good work we do not stone

You, but for blasphemy; and because You, being a man, make Yourself out to be God.'" (10:31-33)

The Jews were outraged when Jesus said He was one with God. They were ready to throw stones at Him. They believed that He insulted the God they worshipped. If they had realized that the good works that Jesus did could not be done with human power, they would have known that God abided with Him. But they were not interested in the good works; they were only fixated with the words "one with God" and saw it as a grave problem. Knowing their hearts, Jesus wisely asked a question that revealed their true hearts: "I showed you many good works from the Father; for which of them are you stoning Me?"

When the Jews recalled one by one, all the things that Jesus did up to that point, they couldn't find any reason to stone Him. So when they couldn't come up with an adequate reply, they argued that He was being blasphemous saying, "Because You, being a man, make Yourself out to be God." The act of being irreverent or insolent toward God is "blasphemy". In the Bible, it is a word used to describe something that is considered desecration.

"Why Do You Accuse Me of Blasphemy?"

"Jesus answered them, 'Is it not written in your Law, "I have said you are gods"? If he called them 'gods,' to whom the word of God came—and the Scripture cannot be broken—what about the one whom the Father set apart as his very own and sent into the world? Why then do you accuse me of blasphemy because I said, "I am God's Son"?'" (10:34-36).

Jesus used the Law, which the Jews vested such power and authority upon, in order to enlighten the Jews. He used the passage from Psalm 82:6, *"I said, 'You are gods, and all of you are sons of the Most High.'"*

Now why did Jesus say, "The Scripture cannot be broken"? The Bible is God's Words of promise to us. God is not human; therefore with whatever He says, there is no fallacy, and no regrets. He always does what He says He will do. And because the Bible is the sincere promise of God, it cannot be broken. Matthew 5:18 says, *"For truly I say to you, until heaven and earth pass away, not the smallest letter or stroke shall pass from the Law until all is accomplished."*

Jesus was saying that it is recorded in the Law that the people "to whom the word of God came", are gods. There are many people in the Bible who received a special revelation from God. God either spoke directly to the chosen person, or spoke to them through dreams. Jacob's eleventh son, Joseph, interpreted the Pharaoh's dream, which no one else could interpret, and then Pharaoh said to his servants, *"Can we find a man like this, in whom is a divine spirit?"* (Genesis 41:38) To Moses, the leader of the Great Exodus, God said, *"See, I make you as God to Pharaoh"* (Exodus 7:1). The apostle Paul also showed many amazing works of God, and people also thought of him as a god (Acts 14:11, 28:6).

When Jesus said, "I and the Father are one", they took that as "claiming to be God". Jesus always called God "Father". He never said, "I am God." Nonetheless, based on the passage from Leviticus 24:16, *"The one who blasphemes the name of the LORD shall surely be put to death; all the congregation shall certainly stone him,"* they thought they found a just reason to kill, according to the Law.

"Though You Do Not Believe Me, Believe the Works"

"'If I do not do the works of My Father, do not believe Me; but if I do them, though you do not believe Me, believe the works, so that you may know and understand that the Father is in Me, and I in the Father.' Therefore they were seeking again to seize Him, and He eluded their grasp." (10:37-39)

Jesus was very heartbroken because of the Jews. Even though He had shown them God's amazing works on many occasions, they still did not believe Him because of the envy and jealousy in their hearts. If they really could not believe, even though they should have believed, Jesus urged them to at least believe the work that He had done by saying, "If I do not do the works of My Father, do not believe Me; but if I do them, though you do not believe Me, believe the works, so that you may know and understand that the Father is in Me, and I in the Father."

The works that Jesus did cannot be done with human power. One can only acknowledge that He did those things with the power of God. Jesus wanted them to have faith at least by seeing those things. This passage captures Jesus' heart—the heart that sincerely longed to save one more soul.

But no matter how much Jesus tried to enlighten them, they just did not understand. The Jews became all the more angry and tried to seize Jesus. However, once again, Jesus wisely eluded their grasp. Yes, it was not yet His time to be captured; but more importantly, Jesus' words carried such dignity and authority that no one could dare come and grab Him.

The People Who Believed Beyond the Jordan

"And He went away again beyond the Jordan to the place where John was first baptizing, and He was staying there. Many came to Him and were saying, 'While John performed no sign, yet everything John said about this man was true.' Many believed in Him there." (10:40-42)

Jesus again went beyond the Jordan. This was the region of Berea, where John the Baptist first baptized. To the people who gathered there after hearing news about Him, Jesus taught the gospel of Heaven and performed many miraculous signs, including healing the sick. When the people in that region directly came in contact with Jesus' Words and His ministry, they said, "While John performed no sign, yet everything John said about this man was true."

The reactions of the people in the Berea region were very

different from the reactions of the Jews in Jerusalem. The good and evil in people's hearts are clearly evident here. Good people try to believe good and kind words that pertain to the truth. Especially when someone justifies his words with signs and wonders like Jesus, they believe. This is because miraculous signs do not occur by human power; it is only possible in God (Psalm 62:11).

About the Author
Dr. Jaerock Lee

Dr. Jaerock Lee was born in Muan, Jeonnam Province, Republic of Korea, in 1943. In his twenties, Dr. Lee suffered from a variety of incurable diseases for seven years and awaited death with no hope for recovery. One day in the spring of 1974, however, he was led to a church by his sister and when he knelt down to pray, the Living God immediately healed him of all his diseases.

From the moment Dr. Lee met the Living God through that wonderful experience, he has loved God with all his heart and sincerity, and in 1978 he was called to be a servant of God. He prayed fervently so that he could clearly understand the will of God, wholly accomplish it and obey all the Words of God. In 1982, he founded Manmin Central Church in Seoul, Korea, and countless works of God, including miraculous healings and wonders, have been taking place at his church.

In 1986, Dr. Lee was ordained as a pastor at the Annual Assembly of Jesus' Sungkyul Church of Korea, and four years later in 1990, his sermons began to be broadcast in Australia, Russia, the Philippines, and many more through the Far East Broadcasting Company, the Asia Broadcast Station, and the Washington Christian Radio System.

Three years later in 1993, Manmin Central Church was selected as one of the "World's Top 50 Churches" by the *Christian World* magazine (US) and he received an Honorary Doctorate of Divinity from Christian Faith College, Florida, USA, and in 1996 a Ph. D. in Ministry from Kingsway Theological Seminary, Iowa, USA.

Since 1993, Dr. Lee has been spearheading world evangelization through many overseas crusades in Tanzania, Argentina, L.A., Baltimore City, Hawaii, and New York City of the USA, Uganda, Japan, Pakistan, Kenya, the Philippines, Honduras, India, Russia, Germany, Peru, Democratic Republic of the Congo, Israel and Estonia. In 2002 he was called a "worldwide revivalist" by major Christian newspapers in Korea for his powerful ministries in various overseas crusades. Especially, his 'New York

Crusade 2006' held in Madison Square Garden, the most world-famous arena, was broadcast to 220 nations, and in his 'Israel United Crusade 2009' held in International Convention Center in Jerusalem he boldly proclaimed Jesus Christ is the Messiah and Savior. His sermon is broadcast to 176 nations via satellites including GCN TV and he was listed as one of the Top 10 Most Influential Christian Leaders of 2009 and 2010 by the Russian popular Christian magazine In Victory and new agency Christian Telegraph for his powerful TV broadcasting ministry and overseas church-pastoring ministry.

As of June of 2012, Manmin Central Church has a congregation of more than 120,000 members. There are 10,000 branch churches throughout the globe including 56 domestic branch churches, and so far more than 129 missionaries have been commissioned to 23 countries, including the United States, Russia, Germany, Canada, Japan, China, France, India, Kenya, and many more.

As of the date of this publishing, Dr. Lee has written 64 books, including bestsellers *Tasting Eternal Life before Death, My Life My Faith I & II, The Message of the Cross, The Measure of Faith, Heaven I & II, Hell,* and *The Power of God.* His works have been translated into more than 73 languages.

His Christian columns appear on *The Hankook Ilbo, The JoongAng Daily, The Chosun Ilbo, The Dong-A Ilbo, The Munhwa Ilbo, The Seoul Shinmun, The Kyunghyang Shinmun, The Hankyoreh Shinmun, The Korea Economic Daily, The Korea Herald, The Shisa News,* and *The Christian Press.*

Dr. Lee is currently leader of many missionary organizations and associations: including Chairman, The United Holiness Church of Jesus Christ; President, Manmin World Mission; Permanent President, The World Christianity Revival Mission Association; Founder & Board Chairman, Global Christian Network (GCN); Founder & Board Chairman, World Christian Doctors Network (WCDN); and Founder & Board Chairman, Manmin International Seminary (MIS).

Heaven I & II

A detailed sketch of the gorgeous living environment the heavenly citizens enjoy and beautiful description of different levels of heavenly kingdoms.

The Message of the Cross

A powerful awakening message for all the people who are spiritually asleep! In this book you will find the reason Jesus is the only Savior and the true love of God.

Hell

An earnest message to all mankind from God, who wishes not even one soul to fall into the depths of Hell! You will discover the never-before-revealed account of the cruel reality of the Lower Grave and Hell.

Tasting Eternal Life Before Death

A testimonial memoirs of Dr. Jaerock Lee, who was born again and saved from the valley of death and has been leading an exemplary Christian life.

The Measure of Faith

What kind of a dwelling place, crown and reward are prepared for you in Heaven? This book provides with wisdom and guidance for you to measure your faith and cultivate the best and most mature faith.

Awaken, Israel

Why has God kept His eyes on Israel from the beginning of the world to this day? What kind of His providence has been prepared for Israel in the last days, who await the Messiah?

My Life My Faith I & II

Dr. Jaerock Lee's autobiography provides the most fragrant spiritual aroma for the readers, through his life extracted from the love of God blossomed in midst of the dark waves, cold yoke and the deepest despair.

The Power of God

A must-read that serves as an essential guide by which one can possess true faith and experience the wondrous power of God